THE FACILITY MANAGER'S GUIDE TO ENVIRONMENTAL HEALTH AND SAFETY

Brian J. Gallant

Government Institutes

An imprint of

THE SCARECROW PRESS, INC.

Lanham, Maryland • *Toronto* • *Plymouth, UK*

2008

Illustrations for the NFPA 704 labeling system, NFPA 704 explanations, business continuity, and outsourcing tips used by permission, © Lab Safety Supply, Janesville, WI.

 **Government Institutes**

Published in the United States of America
by Government Institutes, an imprint of The Scarecrow Press, Inc.
A wholly owned subsidiary of
The Rowman & Littlefield Publishing Group, Inc.
4501 Forbes Boulevard, Suite 200
Lanham, Maryland 20706
http://www.govinstpress.com/

Estover Road
Plymouth PL6 7PY
United Kingdom

British Library Cataloguing in Publication Information Available

Library of Congress Cataloging-in-Publication Data

Gallant, Brian.
  The facility manager's guide to environmental health and safety / Brian J. Gallant.
    p. ; cm.
  ISBN-13: 978-0-86587-187-8 (pbk. : alk. paper)
  ISBN-10: 0-86587-187-6 (pbk. : alk. paper)
  1. Occupational health—United States. 2. Environmental health—United States. 3. Industrial safety—United States. 4. Facility management—United States. I. Title. [DNLM: 1. Occupational Health—United States. 2. Environmental Health—organization & administration—United States. 3. Facility Regulation and Control—organization & administration—United States. 4. Hazardous Waste—prevention & control—United States. 5. Health Policy—United States. 6. Safety Management—organization & administration—United States. WA 400 G166f 2008]
  RC967.G34 2008
  362.196'9800973—dc22   2007031697

Contents

List of Figures

Preface

THE PURPOSE OF THIS BOOK IS to provide facility managers (new and existing) with an overview of environmental, health, and safety issues. By no means are facility managers expected to be health and safety experts, nor do they generally conduct comprehensive worksite safety inspections for regulatory compliance, even though some facility managers might perform them. However, a basic appreciation of the environmental, health, safety, and regulatory issues most frequently encountered in most companies will help ensure a safe work environment for company employees and contractors and minimize potential liability exposures.

This book does not cover every regulation covered by the Occupational Safety and Health Administration, the Environmental Protection Agency, the Department of Transportation, and other regulatory agencies that your company may have dealings with, but instead serves as a guidance book for the major regulations.

The included information, checklists, forms, and recommendations are for general guidance only and should not be relied upon for legal compliance purposes. They are based solely on the information provided to me and relate only to those conditions specifically discussed. I do not make any warranty, expressed or implied, that your workplace is safe or healthful or that it complies with all laws, regulations, and standards.

This book would not have been possible without the help and support of many people. To the many students that I have had in class over the years, I thank you for your attention and ideas. Thanks to my brother, Dick, and his family for all the help they have always provided to me. Thanks, also to my mother-in-law, Ellen, who has been so encouraging and supporting. I appreciate all of you. Last, but certainly not least, special thanks go to my wife, Heather. She has undoubtedly been my biggest fan and one who has helped with this project from start to finish. Thank you, honey, for all your support and especially your love.

1

What Are the Roles and Responsibilities of Facility Managers?

THE ROLE OF A FACILITY MANAGER IS CHANGING RAPIDLY in today's workplace. The shift to a more global workforce is driving many companies to create competitive advantages through cutting-edge technologies. Additionally, companies are combining job duties and eliminating some redundant or overlapping manager duties. This puts a strain on the facility manger and will continue to do so in the near future.

Today's facility manager has to deal with a number of issues affecting the workplace that his or her predecessors did not have to face. These include the following:

- Workplace strategies
- Organizational operations/concerns
- Change management
- Risk management
- Real estate/acquisitions/sales
- Maintenance concerns
- Environmental concerns
- Energy conservation (renewable energy)
- Recycling
- Waste management/hazardous materials
- Human relations
- Ergonomics
- Heating, ventilation, and air-conditioning
- Indoor air quality
- Safety and health
- New technologies/emerging issues

In most companies, the responsibilities of facility managers are diverse, depending on the business nature of the company. However, the most common goal is to maximize the productivity level within the company by utilizing the most cost-effective means. Since a sizeable amount of companies recruit a facility manager when their properties start to go beyond their ability to handle the facilities, in terms of an expansion or possibly a reduction, they will look for the most qualified person with an ability to absorb many of the tasks that are listed previously. We are seeing more and more facility managers with multiple certifications and/or degrees. Managers are responsible for operations and maintenance management, including managing processes, procedures and practices, equipment, and workspace programs. Financial management is also a critical feature for the facility manager in today's world. Anticipating and managing the facilities' operating, administrative, and project budgets are all factors that will definitely need to be considered.

Depending on the specific needs of the company, knowledge of a specific field rather than an overall knowledge in facility management is not usually preferred, as mentioned earlier. Required management skills include strategic planning, space planning, workspace specification and installation, new construction, renovation, project management, tenant improvement design, and implementation management.

The titles being used to describe the facilities manager may vary from company to company, but include:

- Building Maintenance Supervisor
- Convention Center Manager
- Facilities Space and Planning Manager
- Facilities/Site Manager
- Strategic Planning Manager
- Facilities Engineer/Manager

FIGURE 1.1
Massachusetts Maritime Academy Building

- Programmer
- Analyst

These terms may stem from the various major task characteristics that the company expects to be achieved by the facilities manager they choose to hire. The title is not what is important—it's the worker selected to fill the job that counts. I often say, "Call me anything—but pay me what I'm worth."

The facility manager's role is constantly expanding. Facility managers are no longer just in charge of the building maintenance of businesses, but rather facility managers are playing key roles in the critical operations of businesses. Programs at large and small colleges and universities around the country have introduced bachelor's and master's degrees for facility managers who want to be specifically educated in this emergent and diversifying field. Massachusetts Maritime Academy (figure 1.1) recently implemented a graduate program in Facilities Management and is even considering offering the program online. The online option will allow those individuals who have hectic schedules or travel commitments to obtain a master's degree. Times are certainly changing!

From working as a facility manager in a "universal" company to working in a facilities management consulting firm, to working in other associated fields, such as architecture and interior design, the facility manager has, without a doubt, moved from the janitor's closet to the executive board room (see figure 1.2).

While the basic role of a facility manager is very similar, the experience varies with each assignment, as various businesses carry their own unique needs and desires.

FIGURE 1.2
Facility manager at work

FIGURE 1.3
EHS symbol

Recent changes in the economic and business climate have put significant additional pressures on the facilities management profession, making it even more demanding and challenging. As budgets shrink and responsibilities expand, facility managers find themselves on a roller coaster ride of trying to hold their departments together and justify their activities to upper-level management. In addition to the previously described duties, such as daily operations, budgeting, new construction, and project management, today's facility manager also handles maintenance, renovations, and environmental health and safety (EHS) issues for the company. Most of these tasks have been covered in one or more college courses. The EHS piece is one that will be discussed further in this book (also see figure 1.3).

Facility managers need to measure progress through lessons learned, and one of the main lessons learned is that as the role of the facility manager evolves, he or she needs to develop new skills, especially with respect to the dynamic EHS responsibilities. Some important skills for today's facility manager include:

- Business skills: to show the value of and build EHS activities into the company's business plans
- Communication skills: to make EHS understandable to all levels of the company
- Project management skills: to build user-friendly management systems that will make the job easier and more efficient

Facility managers need to be skilled in managing change as well. Not surprisingly, facility managers are faced with increased workloads and more departments reporting to them. Technology has had a profound impact on the business world, changing the way companies work. Additionally, facility managers will also need to consider the regulatory climate and increased security needs as a top issue in the years to come. The events of September 11, 2001, have changed attitudes toward security and altered what is expected of the facilities managers.

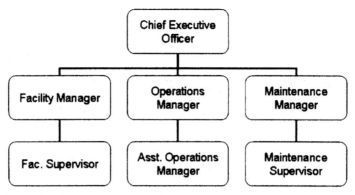

FIGURE 1.4
Organization chart showing facility manager

Reporting directly to senior management (see figure 1.4), facility managers are tasked with driving forward the company's goals through the care of the largest corporate expense: the building (facility) itself. As discussed, this has led to an expansion of duties within the field and created a balancing act for facility managers. They must handle their traditional responsibilities and the newly adopted ones. The facility manager's uniform includes not only wearing work boots and possessing successful engineering skills but also wearing shirts and ties and having confident business insight.

More Responsibilities

Some years ago, the nation's economy forced companies into a withdrawal phase, and many organizations were forced to downsize in an attempt to correct their financial woes and remain in business. With this in mind, facility managers have compensated by taking on duties in which they had no prior educational training or job experience—EHS is an example!

With more duties, buildings, and people reporting to them, without a doubt, facility professionals are busier than ever before.

Responsibilities Include Environmental Health and Safety Activities

Prevention of accidental injuries and losses is part of a company's everyday operations. No aspect of the operation of Facilities Management should take precedence over the safety of its employees. It is expected that all employees, workers and managers alike, strive to create and maintain a safe working environment for everyone by following all established safety procedures, policies, and programs and by actively participating in the identification, reporting, and correction of any hazardous situations.

The Chain of Responsibility

Responsibility for safety is best described as a chain, which is only as strong as its weakest link. For this to be effective, each and every person in the chain has to adhere to a common strategy, which is: Your first recourse when dealing with safety matters is always your immediate supervisor.

The employee's responsibilities include, but are not limited to the following:

- To conduct work in a manner that will not endanger yourself, coworkers, or other employees of the company
- To follow safety procedures, policies, programs, and instructions, including those described in the OSHA regulations and the company's safety manual
- To cooperate with the Safety Committee and any of its members
- To participate in the identification and correction of hazards by alerting your supervisor as soon as possible of any accidents, injuries, or hazardous situations you may encounter

The supervisor's responsibilities include, but are not limited to the following:

- To inform workers of the safe work methods and protective equipment needed for a particular task
- To inspect work areas under his or her control
- To report accidents, dangerous incidents, and hazardous situations in a timely manner
- To take the necessary steps to correct hazards as soon as possible

The Safety Committee's responsibilities include, but are not limited to the following:

- To assist in the development of safety standards and procedures for the company
- To review and analyze accidents and dangerous incidents
- To promote safety awareness
- To serve as a problem-solving forum for addressing safety issues affecting the company's operations, as well as maintenance issues as they relate to the safety of the company
- To recommend and participate in the implementation of company safety activities, such as education and training, inspections, and safety reviews

The facility manager's responsibilities include, but are not limited to the following:

- To provide advice, information, and training related to safety in the workplace
- To perform measurement and evaluation of work-related hazards
- To act as liaison between the company and government or regulatory agencies involved in health and safety affairs
- To collect and dispose of hazardous wastes (oils, solvents, acids, bases, radioactive materials, laboratory chemicals, etc.)
- To provide assistance in the event of accidental spills, leaks, or releases of hazardous materials
- To supervise decontamination projects, such as underground tank removal or similar tasks

Safety: Who's Responsible?

The age-old saying is that everyone is responsible for his or her own safety. While this is obviously a true statement, as facility managers, we certainly have a greater responsibility to the

FIGURE 1.5
EPA logo

company and its employees due to our role and responsibilities in the EHS arena. Department heads, managers, directors of programs, supervisors, foremen, and so on, all share responsibility for the health and safety of individuals engaged in activities under their direction or supervision. They are obliged to make sure that the activities of these individuals comply with all relevant regulations (federal, state, and local), accepted standards, and best practices, and that work activities are performed in a safe and thoughtful manner.

Every employee is also responsible for complying with all of the applicable provisions of environmental, health, and safety standards and regulations (EPA, OSHA, etc.). They also must abide by all company and departmental or office safety policies and procedures and comply with safety directives issued by their individual supervisors. These are all pretty tall orders, but nevertheless, they must be followed. Figure 1.5 displays an EPA logo.

You might be thinking, "How do I know what all of the environmental, health, and safety standards are?" That is a difficult question to answer, regardless of whether the facility manager has a background in EHS. This book will hopefully help educate facility managers in this regard. However, please remember that ignorance of the regulations doesn't excuse you or your company from compliance with them.

Housekeeping

- Good housekeeping is an essential part of every job (see figure 1.6). Work areas, aisles, walkways, and equipment shall be kept clear of loose materials, tools, refuse, and scrap material.

- Materials, such as lumber and pipe, shall be stored in an orderly and secure manner away from high pedestrian traffic areas.
- Compressed gases, chemical products, or other hazardous materials shall not be left unattended in public areas. Gas cylinders, whether full or empty, should always be secured to a wall, bench, or rack.
- Spills, such as grease, water, or oil, shall be cleaned up as soon as possible; a delay could result in an accident to you or a fellow worker. If assistance from hazardous materials technicians is required, call the security dispatcher.
- A safe access shall be maintained to work areas. Shortcuts, such as through construction areas, should be avoided. Never block aisles, traffic lanes, or fire exits with equipment or materials, and make sure members of the public are kept out of hazardous work areas by way of barricades and signage.
- Restore work areas to their normal condition prior to leaving by replacing ceiling tiles and access panels that may have been removed during the course of your work.

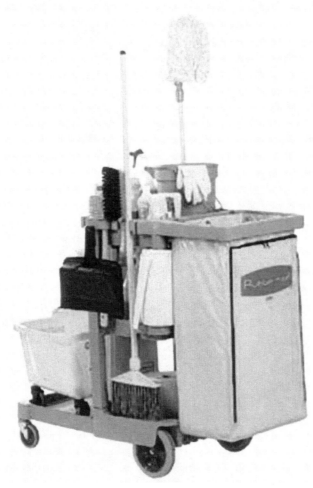

FIGURE 1.6
Good housekeeping

Resources

There are several resources available to provide information, consultation, and other services as needed. You may have some internal company personnel with particular expertise in health and safety-related issues. The Internet is always available for researching various issues that may arise. Included in the Appendix A are the Regional Office contacts for both OSHA and EPA. Trade journals, industry associations, and networking with peers are all valuable resources for the facility manager.

2

Introduction to the Occupational Safety and Health Administration

THE OCCUPATIONAL SAFETY AND HEALTH ACT (OSHAct) of 1970 was passed by the United States Congress "to assure, so far as possible, every working man and woman in the Nation safe and healthful working conditions and to preserve our human resources" (see www.osha.gov). Under the OSHAct, OSHA was established as an agency within the Department of Labor and was authorized to regulate health and safety conditions for all employers with a few exceptions (certain federal agencies and farms at which only family members are employed, etc.).

The OSHAct

The OSHAct of 1970 requires that every employer covered under the act furnish to all employees a place of employment that is free from recognized hazards that are causing or likely to cause death or serious physical harm (injury) to the employees.

In addition, the act requires that employers comply with occupational safety and health standards published under the act, and that employees comply with standards, rules, regulations, and orders issued under the act that are applicable to their own actions and business operations.

Under the OSHAct, OSHA was created for the following purposes:

- To encourage employers and employees to reduce workplace hazards and to implement new or improve existing safety and health standards
- To provide for research in occupational safety and health and develop innovative ways of dealing with occupational safety and health problems
- To establish "separate but dependent responsibilities and rights" for employers and employees for the achievement of better safety and health conditions
- To maintain a reporting and recordkeeping system to monitor job-related injuries and illnesses
- To establish training programs to increase the number and competence of occupational safety and health personnel
- To develop mandatory job safety and health standards and enforce them effectively

FIGURE 2.1
OSHA logo

OSHA Standards

The OSHA standards affecting the majority of companies fall into two major categories: (1) general industry and (2) construction. These standards may require the adoption or use of one or more practices, means, methods, or processes reasonably necessary or appropriate to provide protection on the job. In many companies, it is the facility manager's responsibility to become familiar with the applicable standards for his or her type of business and to ensure that employees follow procedures, including the use of personal protective equipment as required.

General Duty Clause

Every situation is different! Companies perform different tasks and employees do different jobs. Think of all the various industries that exist and imagine how tough it must be to write OSHA standards for each and every task, company, and situation. It's impossible.

Where OSHA has not promulgated specific standards to address a given situation, employers are responsible for following the intent of OSHAct's general duty clause. The general duty clause states that each employer shall furnish "a place of employment which is free from recognized hazards that are causing or are likely to cause death or serious physical harm to its employees." In those cases where a specific standard does not exist, OSHA will use the general duty clause for the issuance of citations and fines. For situations in which the so-called gray areas are present and you may be trying to convince yourself that there is no OSHA regulation for a certain task or job, please remember the general duty clause.

Development and Adoption of Standards

How do we get OSHA standards? The standard-setting procedure can be started in several different ways. OSHA can simply begin the process on its own initiative or in response to petitions from private citizens or other parties. Once OSHA has developed plans to propose, amend, or delete a standard, it publishes these intentions in the Federal Register as a Notice of Proposed Rulemaking or often as an Advanced Notice of Proposed Rulemaking. The notice will include the terms of the new rule and provide a specific time for the public to respond. Interested parties may submit written comments or arguments and pertinent evidence and may request a public hearing on the proposal if none had been announced in the notice.

After the close of the comment period or public hearing, OSHA must then publish, in the Federal Register, the full, final text of the adopted standard and the date the standard will become effective, along with an explanation of the standard and the reasons for implementing it.

FIGURE 2.2
OSHA standards book

Keeping Employees Informed: It's Your Responsibility

Companies are responsible for keeping employees informed and up-to-date about OSHA and about the various safety and health matters with which they are involved. It is an often overlooked task for facility managers due to the ever-increasing workload, but keeping employees educated about OSHA will pay dividends later. This task may ultimately fall upon the facility manager to implement, because of the dealings they have with the regulations. OSHA requires that each company post certain materials in a prominent location in the workplace. These items include:

- Job Safety and Health Protection (federal workplace poster): This poster (figure 2.3) informs employees of their rights and responsibilities under the OSHAct (typically, this is a free item from OSHA or it can be downloaded and printed out on your printer).
- Some states also require additional postings. Check with your local OSHA office or state labor agency to determine if you need any other postings.

FIGURE 2.3
The required OSHA poster

- Summaries of petitions for variances from standards or recordkeeping procedures.
- Copies of OSHA citations for violations of standards (figure 2.4): These must remain posted at or near the location of the alleged violations for three days or until the violations are abated, whichever is longer.

The third bulleted item above (summaries of petitions for variances) is only if the company has applied for and/or received a variance for a particular standard. The fourth bulleted item above (copies of OSHA citations) applies only if the company receives a citation from OSHA.

It is far better to keep employees informed about their rights and responsibilities with respect to OSHA than to have a disgruntled employee call OSHA and file a complaint needlessly. Employees need to know and be constantly reassured that the company cares about each and every employee's safety.

Occasionally, OSHA standards or NIOSH (National Institute for Occupational Safety and Health) research activities will require an employer to measure and/or record employee exposures to potentially harmful substances (hazardous materials or chemical substances). Employ-

State of California
Division of Occupational Safety and Health
West Covina District Office (0950644; 4044)
1906 West Garvey Avenue South, Suite 200
West Covina, CA 91790

Inspection Number: ████████
Inspection Dates: 01/31/2002 -
Issuance Date: 07/10/2002
CSHO ID: ████████
Optional Inspection Nbr: ████████

Citation and Notification of Penalty

Company Name: ████████
Inspection Site: ████████████████████████

Citation 2 Item 1 Type of Violation: **Serious**

California Code of Regulations, Title 8, Section 3203
(a) Effective July 1, 1991, every employer shall establish, implement and maintain an effective Injury and Illness Prevention Program (Program). The Program shall be in writing and, shall, at a minimum:
(6) Include methods and/or procedures for correcting unsafe or unhealthy conditions, work practices and work procedures in a timely manner based on the severity of the hazard:
(A) When observed or discovered; and,
(B) When an imminent hazard exists which cannot be immediately abated without endangering employee(s) and/or property, remove all exposed personnel from the area except those necessary to correct the existing condition. Employees necessary to correct the hazardous condition shall be provided the necessary safeguards.

Violation:
On the date a serious accident occurred, 1/11/02, the employer had not established and implemented an effective Injury, Illness Prevention Program (IIPP). A procedure for correcting unsafe or unhealthy conditions, work practices and work procedures was not implemented nor was it included in the written IIPP. The employer had identified the hazard approx. 2 years earlier when the curtain was installed but had not corrected the hazard in a timely manner.

Date By Which Violation Must be Abated: 07/20/2002
Proposed Penalty: $ 18000.00

signature — ADM
Compliance Officer/District Manager

See pages 1 through 4 of this Citation and Notification of Penalty for information on employer and employee rights and responsibilities.

Citation and Notification of Penalty   Page 10 of 11.   CalOSHA - 2 (9-97)

FIGURE 2.4
An OSHA violation

ees have the right (in person or through their authorized representative—union representative, lawyer, or doctor) to be present during the measuring process and to examine records of the results. Each employee or former employee has the right to see his or her examination records and must be told if his or her exposure has exceeded the levels set by the OSHA standards. The employee must also be told what corrective actions are being (or will be) taken to address the conditions found.

Workplace Inspections

Hopefully, your company will never experience an OSHA inspection. There are a few things facility managers should know about what takes place and how to respond when this does happen. OSHA is authorized to conduct workplace inspections to enforce its standards. All

FIGURE 2.5
An OSHA inspection violation depicted

establishments covered under the OSHAct, likely including your company, are subject to inspection by OSHA compliance safety and health officers.

Consistent with the OSHAct, an OSHA compliance officer is authorized to:

- "Enter without delay and at reasonable times any factory, plant, establishment, construction site or other areas, workplace, or environment where work is being performed by an employee of the employer."
- "Inspect and investigate during regular working hours, and at other reasonable times, and within reasonable limits and in a reasonable manner, any such place of employment and all pertinent conditions, structures, machines, apparatus, devices, equipment and equipment therein, and to question privately any such employer, owner, operator, agent or employee."

Nearly all these inspections are conducted without any advanced notice. However, when advance notice of an inspection is given, the employer must inform his or her employees' representatives or arrange for OSHA to do so. OSHA usually does not have a warrant for an inspection when they first arrive and may not conduct an inspection (without a warrant) without an employer's consent. OSHA compliance officers may, however, inspect after acquiring a search warrant or its equivalent based on administrative probable cause (see figure 2.5).

If an OSHA Compliance Officer Inspects Your Company

If an OSHA Compliance Officer, or other inspector from a regulatory agency, contacts anyone at your facility via phone or mail, he or she should be instructed to notify the facility manager

FIGURE 2.6
An OSHA conference taking place

(if you are in charge of this area). The facility manager will assist the employees/departments involved in determining what steps, if any, need to be taken. If an OSHA Compliance Officer arrives at your facility to conduct an inspection, the procedures described next are highly recommended.

Ask the Compliance Officer for his or her credentials—a badge or photo identification card specifying that the person is an agent of OSHA. This is expected by a compliance officer and won't be considered as a snub. Do not accept a business card as a credential. Anyone can have or make a business card. In addition to the business card, make sure you see the official badge or photo identification card.

Ask whether the Compliance Officer has a warrant for the inspection. Do not demand a warrant; simply inquire whether one exists. Compliance officers have the ability to obtain search warrants to inspect a property or facility. While one is not needed for them to inspect your facility, it is nice to know if one exists. Access to the facility (if a warrant does not exist) can be denied, but before you deny access to any regulatory official, you may want to consult with the company's legal counsel or an attorney in the event that the compliance officer has a warrant.

Before the actual inspection, the Compliance Officer will conduct an opening conference (see figure 2.6), during which the Compliance Officer explains why he or she is there and what he or she wishes to do (the plan of attack, so to speak). It is perfectly alright to ask the Compliance Officer to wait while you assemble the appropriate people for the opening conference. Again, this is not an unusual request (to request that he or she waits) and is expected by the Compliance Officer. You may also want to contact your safety consultant, if you utilize one, and you can ask to wait until this person arrives as well. Regulatory officials are used to the fact that not everyone will be in a position (all at once) to attend the meeting.

FIGURE 2.7
File cabinet for OSHA record-keeping

Contact the plant manager and owner (or similar-titled person in your company) to inform him or her about the arrival of the Compliance Officer. During the waiting period, my recommendation is: Do not leave the Compliance Officer alone with records, documents, safety plans, or procedures. There is plenty of time to review these documents during the inspection process. At no time should you ever tell a Compliance Officer to "help themselves" to the filing cabinets (see figure 2.7).

Do not begin the opening conference without a representative from senior management present (or at least inform them of the conference).

After the opening conference, the Compliance Officer will conduct a walk-around inspection (figure 2.8). The facility manager and any department representative, if applicable, should accompany the Compliance Officer during the inspection. If affected employees in the company are represented by a union, ask employees to designate a union representative to be present during the inspection and accompany the group. This person may be a safety committee person, shop steward, or business agent. If the Compliance Officer wants to observe a certain process or a particular area, take the most direct route to get there and avoid areas of the facility that may expose deficiencies or housekeeping issues, if at all possible, for obvious reasons. It should not be your goal to unnecessarily raise potential to any Compliance Officer.

After the inspection, the facility manager and senior management should meet to discuss the outcome and plan for action, as needed. A closing conference is also held, and the Compliance Officer discusses the inspection, what he or she observed, and any possible findings or areas that may need further attention or corrective actions. Any issue that you can take immediate corrective action on should be handled and documented.

FIGURE 2.8
An OSHA inspection tour

If a notice of violation is issued or received, it must be posted at or near the area of the offense for at least three days, or until the hazard has been eliminated, whichever is longer.

Any fines that may be issued by the OSHA Area Director are the responsibility of the company. My recommendation is that you consult with senior management, your safety consultant, and the company's legal staff or attorney before paying any fines. It may be wise to appeal the violation and discuss ways to implement a program of corrective action. Oftentimes, OSHA may lower the fines and agree to the corrective action plan or may offer one of their own for your consideration. OSHA will also consider your previous safety record, the condition of the facility, and the seriousness of the hazard(s) involved, among other things, when handing down the decision on fines/violations.

In order to have the most "effective" inspection, the following suggestions should be considered by Facility Managers:

- Answer any and all questions truthfully, without directly admitting guilt.
- Never knowingly give false statements or intentionally mislead a Compliance Officer.
- If you do not know the answer to a question, explain that you are not certain and that you will look into the matter further, as necessary. Then follow up and get the answer.
- Do not offer any information unless you are asked for it.
- Do not talk about accidents, incidents, or near-miss events that have occurred in the past unless specifically asked to do so.
- Be courteous. Do not be rude to the Compliance Officer or argue with him or her.

- Do not discuss political views regarding OSHA or the federal government or any of its leaders.
- Do not engage in telling the Compliance Officer that you pay his salary.
- Please remember that the OSHA fines do not go into OSHA's budget. These fines go directly into the U.S. General Treasury or, in the case of a state OSHA fine, the state's General Treasury.

OSHA Compliance Does Not Have to Be Complicated

As previously mentioned, OSHA was originally created as an agency under the Department of Labor in the early 1970s to ensure the safety and health of every American worker. Today, the agency is credited with having developed sensible regulations and significantly reducing the number of worksite injuries and fatalities in this country by over 50 percent, according to the Bureau of Labor Statistics (BLS) data (www.bls.gov). This is an even more impressive statistic when you consider there are twice as many people going to work in twice as many workplaces in the United States now than there were in 1971, according to the same data from the BLS (see figure 2.9).

With such a broad range of issues and the complexity of many facility operations, compliance with OSHA's rules and regulations can often be difficult. In the past, people who wanted such information had to make a written request and wait several weeks for the traditional mail delivery. Today, OSHA has a web site (www.osha.gov) that has sped the pace at which informa-

FIGURE 2.9
BLS logo

tion can be received and disseminated to workers, supervisors, and managers. The site can be used for health and safety information, regulations, and compliance issues.

Laws and Regulations

Many people have the perception that OSHA is about locating problems for the sake of finding them. In reality, OSHA employees and inspectors are much more concerned with making sure that work environments are as safe as they can possibly be for the benefit of each and every employee in every company in America.

The best way for facility managers to be sure their workplaces are up to code is to keep up with the rule changes taking place in their specific industries. The Laws and Regulations section of the OSHA web site is where this information can be found. For the public to achieve a clearer understanding of agency rules, OSHA also publishes written clarifications or interpretations of standards on its site. This keeps OSHA from answering the same inquiries repeatedly and assists people who need to know the intended meaning or thought process behind a rule or standard.

The system allows users to search by a specific standard number or within a given time period. If the question is new, there is information on where to send the question and what can be expected in the process of getting an answer.

Help When You Least Expect It

Although some people may think it frightful, forming a relationship with OSHA can be very helpful. For instance, in the wake of the recent devastation from Hurricane Katrina, OSHA rapidly moved information related to the cleanup efforts to the top of its priority list, as did a large number of the affected business owners and facility managers. Information was made available on general hazards associated with the cleanup efforts. Fact sheets related to mold and indoor air quality were also released for those concerned about dealing with these problems in the flooded areas.

OSHA also looks to the community it serves for information on emerging topics. A good way to get involved is to sign up for Quick Takes, the biweekly e-mail memo produced by OSHA. Sign-up is available on the OSHA home page—and best of all, it's a free service! (See www.osha .gov.)

What Could Be on the Horizon?

While it may seem like hazardous problems arise in the workplace on a daily basis (and perhaps they do), keeping informed and up-to-date of changes in standards and practices does not have to be a full-time chore. I realize that you have many other tasks on your list to accomplish in the course of your day! A good way to see what may be around the corner on the agenda at OSHA is to look at the work-related lawsuits against employers. Mold and indoor air quality issues are congesting the court dockets all over the country. While OSHA has only issued informational guides on these topics to date, a close watch should be kept on the regulatory process with respect to these two important issues and other topics that may arise.

It is certain that OSHA will always be a factor in business safety, but what is more important is the facility manager's ability to navigate through the maze of rules to find answers that will lead to a safe and successful environment. Learning how to use the tools at hand may turn out to be the best defense.

Types of Inspections and Priorities

There are five types of inspections that OSHA conducts. These are listed as follows in their order of importance, as determined by OSHA:

1. Imminent Danger: Imminent danger situations are given the highest priority. An imminent danger is any condition where there is reasonable certainty that a danger exists that can be expected to cause death or serious physical harm either immediately or before the danger can be eliminated through normal enforcement procedures. When an imminent danger situation is found, the Compliance Officer will ask the employer to voluntarily abate the hazard and to remove endangered employees from exposure. Should the employer refuse, OSHA will apply to the nearest Federal District Court for legal action to correct the situation.
2. Catastrophic and Fatal Accidents: Second priority is given to the investigation of fatalities and catastrophes resulting in hospitalization of three or more employees from a single incident. (While many feel that this category should be number one on the priority list, it makes sense to correct the imminent danger, as opposed to dealing with the accident that has already taken place. That's not to say that the fatal accident is not important to OSHA, but it is a close second to the imminent danger category.)
3. Employee Complaints: Each employee has the right to request an OSHA inspection when the employee feels that he or she is in imminent danger from a hazard or when he or she feels that there is a violation of an OSHA standard that threatens physical harm. If the employee so requests, OSHA will withhold the employee's name from the employer. This category can quickly become elevated to a top priority, based on the nature of the complaint.
4. Programmed High Hazard Inspections: OSHA establishes programs of inspection aimed at specific high-hazard industries, occupations, or health hazards. Workplaces are selected for inspection on the basis of death, illness and injury rates, employee exposure to toxic substances, and so on.
5. Re-inspections: Establishments cited for alleged serious violations may be re-inspected to determine whether the hazards have been corrected and/or the company has complied with the OSHA regulations.

Citations and Penalties

After the OSHA Compliance Officer reports findings to his or her office, the OSHA Area Director determines what citations, if any, will be issued and what penalties will be proposed. The types of violations and penalties that may be proposed are as follows:

- Other than serious violation: This type of violation has a direct relationship to job safety and health, but it probably would not cause death or serious physical harm. The maximum proposed penalty for this type of violation is $7,000.

- Serious violation: This involves a violation in which there is substantial probability that death or serious physical harm could result, and in which the employer knew, or should have known, of the hazard. The maximum proposed penalty for this type of violation is $7,000.
- Imminent danger situations: These situations are also cited and penalized as serious violations.
- Willful violation: This is a violation that the employer intentionally and knowingly commits. The employer either knows that the operation constitutes a violation, or is aware that a hazardous condition exists and made no reasonable effort to eliminate it. The penalty range for this type of violation is $5,000 to $70,000.
- Repeated violation: This involves a violation of any standard, regulation, rule, or order where, upon re-inspection, another violation of the same previously cited section is found. Repeated violations can bring fines of up to $70,000.
- Failure to abate: Failure to correct any violations may bring civil penalties of up to $7,000 per day for every day the violation continues beyond the prescribed abatement date.

The other regulatory violations and penalties include the following:

- Falsifying records, reports, or applications can bring a fine of $10,000 and/or six months in jail upon conviction; violations of posting requirements can bring civil penalties of up to $7,000.
- Assaulting a Compliance Officer, or otherwise resisting, opposing, intimidating, or interfering with a Compliance Officer in the performance of his or her duties is also a criminal offense, subject to a fine of not more than $5,000 and/or three years in jail.
- Conviction of a willful violation that has resulted in the death of an employee can lead to individual fines of up to $250,000 and/or six months in jail and corporate fines of up to $500,000.

When to Contact OSHA

There are a few instances when the nearest OSHA office must be contacted by the employer. These instances include the following:

- Any workplace fatality.
- Three or more people are injured and require hospitalization from a single incident.
- OSHA must be notified within eight hours and given all the pertinent details, such as: names of individuals injured or dead, nature of accident, to the extent you know the details, time and location of event, company name and representative (and contact information), hospital location, and other relevant information.

Workplace Injuries and Illnesses

One of things that is dreaded the most in the workplace is an employee injury or illness. An injury or illness is classified as work-related only if it arises out of and in the course of employment at your facility. Specific reporting requirements are mandated under most states'

FIGURE 2.10
An ADA-compliant sign

Workers' Compensation Laws and the Federal OSHAct, some of which are described below. Questions about whether an injury or illness is work-related or reportable should be directed to the company's workman's compensation insurance carrier or to the facility's Human Resources manager.

Individuals that do not have work-related injuries or illnesses but need special accommodation in their workplaces may fall under the Americans with Disabilities Act (ADA). For further information on ADA, your Human Resources manager should be consulted (see figure 2.10). While accidents involving outside contractors or other visitors to the company facilities do not fall within the scope of this section, serious injuries to these individuals should be reported as soon as practicable to the facility manager and other appropriate personnel at your workplace for proper documentation.

Medical Evaluation and Treatment

For all major emergencies: Call 911 (see figure 2.11). For postemergency care and all non-emergencies/minor emergencies, individuals with work-related injuries and illnesses should be referred to the company's medical department, nearest hospital, or medical center for evaluation, consultation, appropriate treatment, and/or referral to licensed professional health care providers. Time out of the workplace for a work-related injury or illness must be reported to the facility manager and Human Resources (at least for documentation). For injuries that result from accidental contact with hazardous or toxic substances, the appropriate supervisor

FIGURE 2.11
Call 9-1-1 in an emergency

and the facility manager should be notified. This way, any corrective action that needs to be taken can be done as soon as possible.

Reporting/Notification

The Employer's First Report of Accident, Injury, or Occupational Illness form must be provided to the facility manager as soon as possible, but no later than seven days after an employee's injury or illness. In addition to fulfilling state and federal reporting requirements, this form must be completed to file a claim under Workers' Compensation.

Except for emergencies, employees must report all injuries to their supervisors as soon as possible but, in all cases, prior to leaving the workplace on the day of the injury. If an individual calls from home to report a work-related injury or illness, his or her supervisor should advise the employee to contact the facility manager and the Human Resources manager. If the supervisor is uncomfortable or uncertain about the circumstances surrounding the injury or illness, he or she should also contact the facility manager and the Human Resources manager explaining the concerns.

Workers' Compensation Insurance

The Workers' Compensation program covers all medical costs for work-related injuries and illnesses that are defined as "reasonable and necessary" by the insurance company. Workers'

Compensation may also pay part of the wages lost if the injury or illness requires a prolonged absence from the workplace (check with your insurance provider for details). In addition, rehabilitation services or other similar care may be authorized.

OSHA Record-keeping and Reporting Requirements

Companies are required by the Federal BLS and OSHA to maintain a log of work-related injuries and illnesses. Information collected on the Employer's First Report of Accident, Injury, or Occupational Illness form described earlier is typically used by facility managers to complete the OSHA 300 log.

OSHA has stringent reporting requirements when a work-related accident results in the hospitalization of three or more individuals or a fatality. These types of accidents must also be reported immediately to the facility manager. Failure to report these accidents to OSHA within eight hours may result in substantial OSHA penalties.

3

Regulations, Agencies, and Resources

EMPLOYEE HEALTH AND SAFETY REGULATIONS IN PLACE in today's work environment stem from the end of the 1800s and the mining industry. Due to the high fatality record among mine workers, a series of laws were established to address the issue in about 1870. After the Second World War, health and safety laws grew to encompass many other industries. It wasn't until 1970, when the United States Congress adopted the OSHAct, that specific laws were enacted to protect workers' health and safety.

Regulations

Prior to 1970, effective workplace safety and health regulations did not exist at either federal or state levels. The regulations that did exist were not enforced. Therefore, large numbers of workers experienced workplace illnesses, injuries, and death as a result of unsafe and unhealthy working conditions. In addition to occupational health and safety concerns, our country's facilities were struggling with environmental management of industrial chemical use, disposal, and various pollution issues.

In 1970, Congress established OSHA to ensure safe and healthful work environments in the manufacturing and construction industries. At the same time, the EPA was instituted to oversee resource management. Today, OSHA is the primary guardian of workers' health and safety standards, while EPA continues to protect the public's health, along with regulating the cleanliness and safety of our land, air, and water.

All of your employees need to have at least a basic understanding of the laws and agencies that help regulate some of the hazardous operations that are conducted at our facilities. Understanding the laws and rules that specify the requirements and restrictions for working in hazardous environments and/or conditions requires familiarity with the evolution and interface of the federal acts and agencies that contain the laws. Many other local, state, and federal entities, in addition to the EPA and OSHA, play key roles in writing and enforcing regulations that affect our day-to-day operations, particularly in the area of environmental health and safety.

FIGURE 3.1
DOT logo

The following is a list of some of the federal agencies that regulate the facilities that are engaged in hazardous waste operations:

- EPA
- Department of Labor (DOL), OSHA
- Department of Transportation (DOT) (see figure 3.1)

Managers should also keep in mind that state and local governments also have regulatory agencies that could have some jurisdiction over some of the facility's operations. If there is a question regarding who has the authority, consult your local authorities for further information.

The Environmental Protection Agency

The EPA governs the quality of our environment, including air, land, and water. In addition, EPA administers the regulations that manage hazardous waste. The EPA played a vital role in developing the Hazardous Waste Operations and Emergency Response (HAZWOPER) regulations that are currently in existence for workers' safety at hazardous waste sites and treatment storage and disposal facilities, and for those workers who respond to emergencies involving hazardous materials regardless of the location.

These are a few parts of the EPA regulations that note where some significant environmental acts are incorporated into the regulations. EPA regulations are found in the Code of Federal Regulations (CFR), specifically in 40 CFR.

- 40 CFR 50-99: Clean Air Act
- 40 CFR 100-140 and 400-470: Clean Water Act
- 40 CFR 240-271: Resource Conservation and Recovery Act (RCRA)
- 40 CFR 260-299: Hazardous Waste Management System
- 40 CFR 279: Used Oil Management Standards
- 40 CFR 700-799: Toxic Substance Control Act (TSCA)

Hazardous wastes are identified by the EPA as described in 40 CFR 261. The listed wastes are known waste streams generated by specific processes. According to RCRA, if a waste is not listed, it must be tested to see if it exhibits one or more of the following characteristics (wastes that exhibit the following characteristics are called characteristic waste):

- Ignitable: waste having a flash point of < 140°F, or an ignitable compressed gas, flammable liquid or solid, or oxidizer according to DOT
- Corrosivity: waste with a pH of < 2.0 or > 12.5
- Reactive: wastes that explode or react violently when exposed to water, or that generate toxic gases
- Toxic: waste analyzed using the Toxic Characteristic Leachate Procedure test to check for toxic constituents at levels greater than those specified in the applicable environmental regulations

Table 3.1 outlines some of the EPA levels.

TABLE 3.1
Environmental Protection Agency's
Toxin Waste Limits

Toxin	U.S. EPA Limits (in ppm)
Arsenic	5.0
Cadmium	1.0
Chromium	5.0
Lead	5.0
Mercury	.02

Hazardous Waste Numbers

A four-digit number is given to different wastes by the EPA for identification purposes. They are:

- D001: Ignitable Wastes
- D002: Corrosive Wastes
- D003: Reactive Wastes
- D004-D043: Toxic Wastes
- D008: Lead
- D018: Benzene
- D019: Carbon Tetrachloride

See figure 3.2 for an example of storing ignitable wastes.

FIGURE 3.2
Cabinet holding ignitable wastes

EPA Identification Numbers

If your facility generates hazardous waste, you will likely need to apply for an EPA identification number. A unique EPA 12-digit number is assigned to each waste generator, transporter, and Treatment, Storage, and Disposal Facility (TSDF). The EPA assigns an identification number to each of these entities for tracking purposes. These numbers are put onto a Hazardous Waste Manifest Form (figure 3.3).

Clean Water Act

The Clean Water Act, amended and reauthorized in 1987, has the goal of maintaining or regaining the chemical, physical, and biological integrity of the United States' waters. Both the EPA and the U.S. Army Corps of Engineers have jurisdiction over this act. The Clean Water Act regulates discharge of toxic and nontoxic pollutants into surface waters. The interim goal is to make surface waters usable for such activities as swimming and fishing, with the ultimate goal to eliminate all discharges into surface waters. EPA sets guidelines, and the individual states issue permits through the National Pollutant Discharge Elimination System (NPDES), specifying the types of control equipment and discharges for each facility (see figure 3.4).

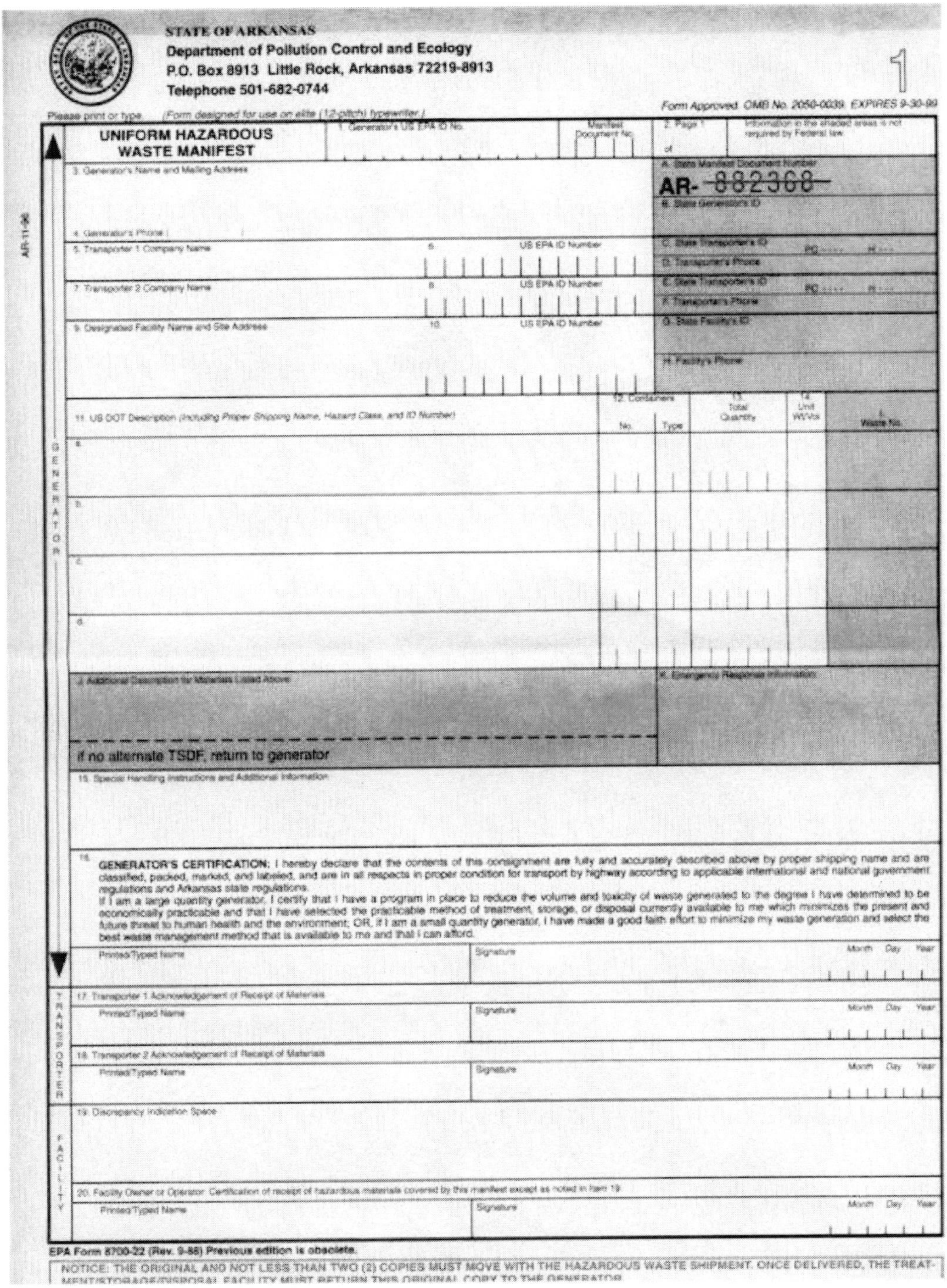

STATE OF ARKANSAS
Department of Pollution Control and Ecology
P.O. Box 8913 Little Rock, Arkansas 72219-8913
Telephone 501-682-0744

1

Please print or type. (Form designed for use on elite (12-pitch) typewriter.)

Form Approved. OMB No. 2050-0039. EXPIRES 9-30-99

UNIFORM HAZARDOUS WASTE MANIFEST

1. Generator's US EPA ID No.

Manifest Document No.

2. Page 1 of

Information in the shaded areas is not required by Federal law.

3. Generator's Name and Mailing Address

A. State Manifest Document Number

AR- 882368

B. State Generator's ID

4. Generator's Phone ( )

5. Transporter 1 Company Name

6. US EPA ID Number

C. State Transporter's ID

D. Transporter's Phone

7. Transporter 2 Company Name

8. US EPA ID Number

E. State Transporter's ID

F. Transporter's Phone

9. Designated Facility Name and Site Address

10. US EPA ID Number

G. State Facility's ID

H. Facility's Phone

11. US DOT Description (Including Proper Shipping Name, Hazard Class, and ID Number)

12. Containers No. Type

13. Total Quantity

14. Unit Wt/Vol

I. Waste No.

a.

b.

c.

d.

J. Additional Descriptions for Materials Listed Above

K. Emergency Response Information

If no alternate TSDF, return to generator

15. Special Handling Instructions and Additional Information

16. GENERATOR'S CERTIFICATION: I hereby declare that the contents of this consignment are fully and accurately described above by proper shipping name and are classified, packed, marked, and labeled, and are in all respects in proper condition for transport by highway according to applicable international and national government regulations and Arkansas state regulations.
If I am a large quantity generator, I certify that I have a program in place to reduce the volume and toxicity of waste generated to the degree I have determined to be economically practicable and that I have selected the practicable method of treatment, storage, or disposal currently available to me which minimizes the present and future threat to human health and the environment; OR, if I am a small quantity generator, I have made a good faith effort to minimize my waste generation and select the best waste management method that is available to me and that I can afford.

Printed/Typed Name | Signature | Month Day Year

17. Transporter 1 Acknowledgement of Receipt of Materials

Printed/Typed Name | Signature | Month Day Year

18. Transporter 2 Acknowledgement of Receipt of Materials

Printed/Typed Name | Signature | Month Day Year

19. Discrepancy Indication Space

20. Facility Owner or Operator: Certification of receipt of hazardous materials covered by this manifest except as noted in Item 19.

Printed/Typed Name | Signature | Month Day Year

GENERATOR — TRANSPORTER — FACILITY

AR-11-96

EPA Form 8700-22 (Rev. 9-88) Previous edition is obsolete.

NOTICE: THE ORIGINAL AND NOT LESS THAN TWO (2) COPIES MUST MOVE WITH THE HAZARDOUS WASTE SHIPMENT. ONCE DELIVERED, THE TREATMENT/STORAGE/DISPOSAL FACILITY MUST RETURN THIS ORIGINAL COPY TO THE GENERATOR.

FIGURE 3.3
Hazardous waste manifest form

FIGURE 3.4
Pipe showing NPDES discharge

Clean Air Act

The Clean Air Act (CAA), reauthorized in 1990, amended the Air Quality Act of 1967. The CAA is designed to enhance the quality of air resources by authorizing the EPA to set the criteria for our nation's air-pollution-control programs. The CAA mandates and enforces toxic emission standards for stationary sources (like power plants and certain facilities) and motor vehicles. Air quality standards are required to be achieved and maintained nationwide for six pollutants. Those six pollutants are:

1. ozone
2. nitrogen dioxide
3. carbon monoxide
4. sulfur dioxide
5. total suspended particulates
6. lead

Resource Conservation and Recovery Act

In the late 1960s and early 1970s, the Congressional Office of Technology Assessment estimated that approximately 250–275 million metric tons of hazardous waste are produced each year in the United States. Air and groundwater pollution, contamination of surface water, and poisoning of animals, as well as humans, by way of the food chain supported the EPA's belief that only a small percentage of generated waste was being disposed of in an environmentally acceptable manner (see figure 3.5).

Congress had generally addressed the problems of solid waste disposal by enacting the Solid Waste Disposal Act in 1965. The first comprehensive federal effort to confront the problems of

FIGURE 3.5
RCRA violation poster

solid and hazardous waste began in 1976, when the Resource Conservation and Recovery Act (RCRA) was enacted. RCRA is an amendment that completely revised the Solid Waste Disposal Act of 1965.

RCRA was established to regulate the management and disposal of hazardous materials and wastes. RCRA gave EPA the authority and responsibility to create and enforce the regulations governing the proper identification, handling, storing, treating, and disposing of hazardous waste. RCRA instituted the manifest system of tracking a hazardous waste from generator through transportation, storage, and disposal. This is often referred to as "cradle-to-grave" liability tracking system. It also encourages hazardous waste recycling and minimization.

As of 1983, an estimated 40 million metric tons of hazardous waste escaped regulatory control through various loopholes in the legislative framework. RCRA was falling short of its intent, and Congress amended it in 1984. These amendments strengthened RCRA to include underground storage tanks (see figure 3.6), redefined small-quantity generator status to include more generators, and restricted liquid and hazardous waste from our nation's landfills.

Toxic Substance Control Act

The Toxic Substance Control Act (TSCA) gave EPA authority to regulate the manufacture, distribution, and use of chemical substances for which there are not specific standards already established. TSCA requires EPA to evaluate chemicals before they are sold, to prevent any unreasonable chemical risk to humans and/or the environment, as well as to create a list of reviewed harmful substances that need precautions and safe work practices when used by facilities or the general public.

Comprehensive Environmental Response Compensation and Liability Act

Enacted to fill a void in the RCRA law, the Comprehensive Environmental Response Compensation and Liability Act (CERCLA) addresses problems associated with contamination from

FIGURE 3.6
An underground storage tank being removed

abandoned facilities, or releases of hazardous substances into the environment from vessels or facilities that are not subject to RCRA's authority. CERCLA, better known to most of us as "The Superfund Legislation," authorizes government money for cleanup of abandoned hazardous waste sites, cleanup and emergency response for transportation incidents involving chemical releases, and payments to injured or affected citizens. This legislation was amended by the Superfund Amendment and Reauthorization Act (SARA) in 1986. Superfund is responsible for the following:

- Established the National Priority List
- Provides for identification and cleanup of hazardous waste sites (see figure 3.7)
- Gets funding to implement these activities from oil tax, waste generator fines, and the United States Treasury (taxpayers)

Superfund Amendment and Reauthorization Act

The Superfund Amendment and Reauthorization Act (SARA) was passed to protect the safety and health of personnel working in hazardous operations, as well as the community at large. First, SARA reauthorized the funding to continue site characterization (assessment) to determine which locations belong on the National Priority List, and also continued abandoned-site cleanup.

In addition, SARA mandated that OSHA establish worker health and safety standards for employees working in hazardous waste operations and all emergency response activities involving

FIGURE 3.7
A Superfund site

FIGURE 3.8
Drums lined up at a treatment storage disposal facility

hazardous materials. SARA required training for both workers and management personnel covering safety and health risks at waste sites, TSDFs (see figure 3.8), and emergency response operations. SARA also initiated the requirement for local and regional emergency contingency planning.

Three distinct titles or sections make up SARA. Titles I and III cover hazardous waste operations, emergency response, and planning, while Title II targets a fund for hazardous waste cleanup activities.

Title I

- Required training for hazardous waste operation site workers and emergency response personnel (HAZWOPER)
- Required preparation of a written emergency response plan for operations in which hazardous materials may be spilled or released
- Required proper procedures for handling emergency response activities

Title II

- Gave authority for Superfund to continue to pay for hazardous waste cleanup through a tax on industry

Title III

- Established Community Right-to-Know largely as a result of the widely published 1984 disaster in Bhopal, India, in which a substantial amount of toxic methyl isocyanate escaped from the Union Carbide facility
- Developed "Comprehensive Community Emergency Plans" by Local Emergency Planning Committees (LEPCs) (see figure 3.9)

FIGURE 3.9
LEPC logo from Waltham, Massachusetts

- Reported specific chemical inventory and release information to local fire officials, LEPCs, and the State Emergency Response Commission (SERC) (see figure 3.10)

FIGURE 3.10
Massachusetts SERC logo

- Required facilities storing chemicals to provide the chemical types, quantity on hand, and locations with inventory lists; fees are assessed based on types of substances and quantities involved
- Local fire departments often visit facilities to determine the hazards and ensure compliance with this title (see figure 3.11)

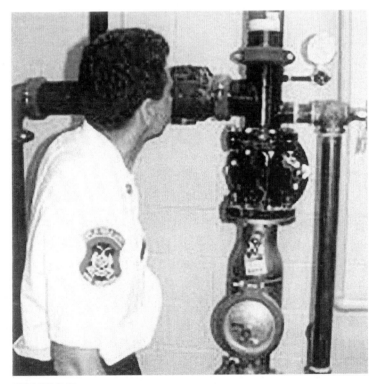

FIGURE 3.11
A fire inspector at a facility

Department of Labor:
Occupational Safety and Health Administration

Under DOL, OSHA is the primary federal agency designated to safeguard the safety and health of the nation's workers in any hazardous activity. OSHA sets, oversees, and enforces health and safety standards for workplace safety. The two most important standards OSHA utilizes to protect employees are the Hazard Communication Standard and the Hazardous Waste Operations and Emergency Response Standard.

Individual states, called "state plan states," may write and enforce their own OSHA regulations, as long as they are at least as stringent as the federal law. States and territories that have their own plan include the following:

- Alaska
- Arizona
- California
- Hawaii
- Indiana
- Iowa
- Kentucky
- Maryland
- Michigan
- Minnesota
- Nevada
- New Mexico
- North Carolina
- Puerto Rico
- Oregon
- South Carolina
- Tennessee
- Utah
- Vermont
- Virgin Islands
- Virginia
- Washington
- Wyoming

The other states fall under the Federal OSHA standards. Keep in mind that the state plans can be stricter than the federal requirements, but they have to meet the federal requirements at a minimum.

National Institute for Occupational Safety and Health

The National Institute for Occupational Safety and Health (NIOSH) is an agency under the Department of Health and Human Services that investigates incidents, researches occupational safety, and recommends exposure limits (RELs) to OSHA for certain hazardous chemicals (see figure 3.12). NIOSH also tests and certifies all respiratory and air sampling devices (except for

FIGURE 3.12
NIOSH logo

mining operations), as well as recommends assigned protection factors (APFs) for respirators. NIOSH does not act in a regulatory capacity at all. They do not issue citations or violations but work very closely with OSHA.

Department of Transportation

The Department of Transportation (DOT) oversees the transport of hazardous materials through interstate commerce. The Hazardous Materials Transportation Act (1975) granted the DOT authority to establish criteria for packaging, labeling, placarding, and shipping papers necessary to transport hazardous materials, as well as the training of personnel responsible for hazardous material transportation. The HMTA was reauthorized in 1990, becoming the Hazardous Materials Transportation Uniform Safety Act (HMTUSA).

The HMTUSA is the federal transportation act that applies to any person or facility that ships hazardous material and/or waste in commerce by air, water, rail, and/or highway. The shipping requirements include preparation of shipping papers or a uniform hazardous waste manifest, placing the material in specific packages, placing the hazard labels on the packages, and placing placards on the shipping containers. Oftentimes the facility manager is responsible for shipping or preparing manifests.

DOT labels are four-inch, diamond-shaped, color-specific stickers that designate the hazard classification of the packaged material (see figure 3.13). Labels are used on nonbulk containers,

FIGURE 3.13
DOT label

FIGURE 3.14
A DOT placard on a truck delivering to a facility

less than or equal to 119 gallons or 882 pounds, along with the shipping name and identification number of the substance in the container.

Placards are 10.7-inch, color-specific diamonds used on freight containers, vehicles, and bulk packages, in addition to the identification number of the material in the container(s) (see figure 3.14). If necessary, placards are required to be placed on each side and on each end of the freight container(s), vehicle(s), and package(s), for a total of four placards of each type on the container.

Both DOT and the United Nations (UN) transportation systems use a four-digit identification number as a reference for substances and materials. If the UN does not have a UN number designated for a material that is considered hazardous under the DOT system, then DOT issues a NA (North America) number. An identification number may be placed in the center of the placard or displayed on packages as part of the hazard identification system. For example, UN 1203 is the identification number for gasoline (figure 3.15).

National Fire Protection Association

While the NFPA has generated several standards, they are not a regulatory or governmental agency. They are a private international group based in Massachusetts. Of particular note to us in the facility management field are the following standards:

- NFPA 704: Labeling
- NFPA 472: Professional Competency of Responders to Hazardous Material Emergencies
- NFPA 1081: Professional Competency of Industrial Fire Brigades

FIGURE 3.15
A 1203 placard (gasoline)

NFPA has many other standards that may have applicability to our industry, but the preceding are most noteworthy.

While the NFPA plays a crucial role in establishing codes and standards on an international basis, again, they are not a governmental or a regulatory agency. Their codes and standards are strictly voluntary; however, many jurisdictions have adopted them and then they become enforceable by those jurisdictions.

NFPA 704 Labeling

The NFPA 704 standard addresses the health, flammability, instability (reactivity), and any related special hazards that may be presented by short-term, acute exposure to a material during handling under conditions of fire, spill, leak, or similar emergencies. It provides four pieces of information to facility workers and also instructions for providing a simple, readily recognized, and easily understood system of markings that provide a general idea of the hazards of chemical materials stored and/or used in an area or space (such a warehouse or production facility) and the severity of these hazards as they relate to handling, fire prevention, exposure, and control.

The hazard ratings reflect the acute effect of a chemical material that involves short-term (minutes or hours), high concentrations, and immediate deleterious health effects (e.g., severe burns, respiratory failure, coma, death, and irreversible damage to a vital organ). Acute exposures are usually related to an accident, such as a chemical spill, massive skin splash, and/or fire. Acute exposures, typically, are sudden and severe and are characterized by rapid absorption of the chemical that is quickly circulated through the body and damage one or more of the vital organs.

The objectives of the NFPA 704 labeling system are:

• To provide an appropriate warning or alert and on-the-spot (immediate) information to safeguard the lives of emergency response personnel (e.g., facility workers, firefighters, HAZMAT responders, or other site workers)

FIGURE 3.16
NFPA 704 label

- To assist in planning for effective fire and hazardous material emergency control operations, including spill cleanup activities
- To assist all designated facility personnel, engineering staff, equipment operators, managers, and safety personnel in evaluating hazards

The NFPA 704 diamond system is intended to provide basic information to fire fighting, emergency, and facility personnel, enabling them to more easily decide whether to evacuate the area or to initiate emergency control procedures. It is also intended to provide them with information to assist in selecting fire fighting tactics, appropriate personal protective equipment, and emergency procedures that may need to be taken.

How is the degree of hazard severity positioned and indicated to reflect potential acute health and/or safety hazard? The NFPA 704 sign (label) consists of four diamonds within a larger diamond (figure 3.16). The red, or flammability, diamond is at "12 o'clock," the yellow, or instability, diamond is at "3 o'clock," the white, or special hazards, diamond is at "6 o'clock," and the blue, or health hazard, diamond is at "9 o'clock."

The degree of hazard severity for a chemical liquid or solid—flammability, health hazard, instability (reactivity)—is indicated by a numerical rating that ranges from four (the most severe hazard) to zero (no significant hazard).

Special hazards are indicated in the white section that is located in the lower region of the 704 sign. There are two special hazard categories:

1. Water reactive: Chemicals that demonstrate unusual reactivity with water are designated by the letter W with a horizontal line through the center (W̶).

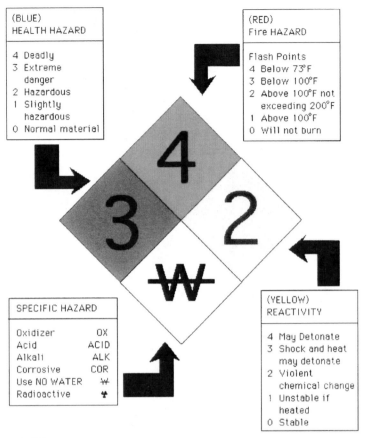

FIGURE 3.17
NFPA 704 system explanations

2. Oxidizers: Chemicals that decompose readily under certain conditions to yield oxygen are designated by the symbol OXY. They may cause a fire in contact with combustible materials, can react violently with water, and can react violently when involved in a fire.

- You may also see other symbols, such as the skull and crossbones for a poison, the radioactive symbol for a radioactive material, and so on.
- This section will not have number, but instead will feature a symbol, words, or a letter to indicate if any special hazard is present (see figure 3.17).

Hazard Communication Standard

The Hazard Communication Standard (Hazcom) or Right-to-Know Law was enacted 1980. We will look at this in-depth in a later chapter. It is also referred to as 29 CFR 1910.1200. The Hazard Communication Standard requires the following:

- Manufacturers and/or importers of chemicals must evaluate the hazards.
- Chemical hazards information must be passed on to employees who have to work with these substances.

MATERIAL SAFETY DATA SHEET — 9 Sections

SECTION 1 — PRODUCT INFORMATION

Product Identifier				WHMIS Classification *(optional)*	
Product Use					
Manufacturer's Name			Supplier's Name		
Street Address			Street Address		
City		Province	City		Province
Postal Code	Emergency Telephone		Postal Code	Emergency Telephone	

SECTION 2 — HAZARDOUS INGREDIENTS

Hazardous Ingredients *(specific)*	%	CAS Number	LD$_{50}$ of Ingredient *(specify species and route)*	LC$_{50}$ of Ingredient *(specify species)*

SECTION 3 — PHYSICAL DATA

Physical State	Odour and Appearance		Odour Threshold (ppm)
Specific Gravity	Vapour Density (air = 1)	Vapour Pressure (mmHg)	Evaporation Rate
Boiling Point (°C)	Freezing Point (°C)	pH	Coefficient of Water/Oil Distribution

SECTION 4 — FIRE AND EXPLOSION DATA

Flammability ☐ Yes ☐ No	If yes, under which conditions?	
Means of Extinction		
Flashpoint (°C) and Method	Upper Flammable Limit (% by volume)	Lower Flammable Limit (% by volume)
Autoignition Temperature (°C)	Explosion Data – Sensitivity to Impact	Explosion Data – Sensitivity to Static Discharge
Hazardous Combustion Products		

SECTION 5 — REACTIVITY DATA

Chemical Stability ☐ Yes ☐ No	If no, under which conditions?
Incompatibility with Other Substances ☐ Yes ☐ No	If yes, which ones?
Reactivity, and under what conditions?	
Hazardous Decomposition Products	

57M2 (R6/99)   SAMPLE FORMAT PROVIDED BY THE WORKERS' COMPENSATION BOARD OF BRITISH COLUMBIA   **Please continue on reverse side**

FIGURE 3.18
An MSDS

- Employees need to know and understand the chemical and physical hazards present in their work environment.

The Hazard Communication Standard also addresses five major topic areas:

1. Hazard determination
2. Written Hazard Communication Program
3. Labels and other forms of warning
4. Material Safety Data Sheets (MSDS) (see figure 3.18)
5. Employee information and training

The Right-to-Know law is one of the top OSHA violations (it is currently the number two violation). The compliance efforts for the employer require a written program, employee training, a workplace inventory of all the hazardous substances, and proper labeling (see figure 3.19). MSDSs need to be kept where employees have ready access to them, and in the event that there is not an MSDS available, the employer has a limited time to provide it to the employee. With the availability of the Internet and fax machines, the employer can usually get the requested MSDS in a short period of time.

FIGURE 3.19
A right-to-know station

Hazardous Waste Operations and Emergency Response

The HAZWOPER regulation (also known as 29 CFR 1910.120) became effective on March 6, 1989, just 18 days prior to the *Exxon Valdez* oil spill in Prince William Sound, Alaska. If your facility deals with hazardous materials or hazardous waste, this regulation may have serious implications for you. A later chapter will explore this topic further.

HAZWOPER requires strict health and safety programs for hazardous waste operations and emergency response operations, as well as the quantity and content of the training that must be provided to anyone who may be exposed to a hazardous waste or material in the workplace.

Contrary to popular belief, HAZWOPER is not just a training regulation. The following sections are included as part of the HAZWOPER standard:

- Scope, Application, and Definitions
- Safety and Health Program
- Site Characterization
- Site Control

- Training
- Medical Surveillance
- Engineering Controls and Personal Protective Equipment
- Monitoring
- Informational Programs
- Handling Drums and Containers
- Decontamination
- Emergency Response
- Illumination
- Sanitation at Temporary Workplaces
- New Technology Programs

HAZWOPER Training

The HAZWOPER Standard is, in my opinion, the most unique OSHA regulation that has been enacted to date. I say that it is unique from two perspectives. They are:

1. There are two training requirements in the one OSHA standard.
2. There is a specification of the number of hours for training personnel.

Just about everything that OSHA deals with has a training implication associated with it. For example, if you operate a forklift, wear a respirator, or enter a confined space (to name just a few things), OSHA requires you to be trained. In most of the regulations, it states that the employer is responsible for training the worker in the particular subject matter or it simply states that the employee will be trained. None of the OSHA regulations (with the exception of the asbestos standard, which, for the most part, EPA enforces) gives us any time frame for the completion of the training with the exception of HAZWOPER (see figure 3.20).

The regulation breaks the training down into two sections. Those are:

1. Hazardous Waste Operations
2. Emergency Response

The training in the hazardous waste operations section is further broken down as follows:

- General Site Workers: These folks need 40 hours of classroom training and 24 hours of on-the-job training (OJT) under a qualified supervisor. People trained at this level include:

  Cleanup workers at hazardous waste sites
  Those personnel removing underground storage tanks and so on.

- Occasional Site Workers: Personnel trained at this level need 24 hours of classroom training and eight hours of OJT, under a qualified supervisor. This certification is needed if you work in any of the following capacities:

  Someone who works at a hazardous waste cleanup site on an occasional basis (such as an engineer)

FIGURE 3.20
The author's HAZWOPER Training Manual

    Project manager
    Surveyor
    Someone who regularly works with, or cleans up hazardous materials or wastes with ex-
        posures within "permissible" levels (PEL) and that do not require the use of respiratory
        protection

- Supervisors: Managers or personnel that supervise others are required to have an addi-
    tional eight hours of training.

Table 3.2 outlines the worker training requirements for the hazardous waste operations workers.
    OSHA also has training requirements for the emergency response workers. They include
these categories:

- First Responder Awareness: The first responder recognizes and identifies hazards and initi-
    ates the response plan. Employees cannot take actions to deal with spills, leaks, or releases.

TABLE 3.2
Worker Training Requirements

Level	Training Requirement
General Site Workers	40 hours and 24 hours on-the-job training
Occasional Site Workers	24 hours and eight hours on-the-job training
Supervisors/Managers	Additional eight hours
Refresher Training	Eight hours annually

- First Responder Operations: Employees can take defensive actions to protect nearby personnel, property, and the environment without putting themselves at risk.
- Hazardous Material Technician: Employees can take offensive, aggressive action to stop a release and contain and control emergency situations. When it comes to emergency response, these individuals are the "gurus."
- Hazardous Material Specialist: These individuals have specialized training or experience in a specific discipline that is necessary to properly mitigate the response. Often, these individuals act as liaisons.
- Incident Commander: These individuals are generally the senior officials on the scene and usually have the highest training (but not necessarily). OSHA states that if you are going to take any action at a spill, leak, or release, then you must have someone in charge. This is that person.

OSHA states that the emergency response training is not a requirement for facility personnel unless the employer expects the employees to perform emergency response duties. Facilities have other options available to them. Some options are:

- Train a group of facility workers (every shift) to respond to hazardous material emergencies.
- Utilize a licensed contractor that is capable to deal with hazardous material/waste to respond to your facility emergencies.
- Call 911 and request assistance from the local fire department.

It should be noted that the emergency response training requirements do not satisfy the hazardous waste operations requirements and vice versa. Table 3.3 highlights the training requirements for those facility staff who will act in the role of emergency response personnel.

TABLE 3.3
Emergency Response Training Requirements

Level	Training Requirement
First Responder Awareness	No specific hours stated
First Responder Operations	Minimum of eight hours
Hazardous Material Technician	Minimum of 24 hours
Hazardous Material Specialist	Skills and knowledge of Hazardous Material Technician and/or education and experience
Incident Commander	Eight hours in addition to at least 24 hours of training at the Operations level

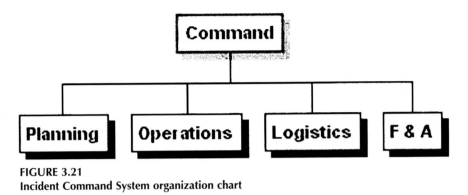

FIGURE 3.21
Incident Command System organization chart

Incident Command System

After the events following September 11, 2001, many facilities established emergency response capabilities or business continuity units. Having a system in place to deal with "who's in charge" is imperative, as once an emergency hits, command and control needs to be established immediately. The Incident Command System (ICS) is a preplanned chain of command used during emergency response. ICS is usually an interface of federal, state, local, and private (facility) industry personnel fulfilling designated roles. Preplanning, training, and practice are required to ensure that everyone knows his or her role within the ICS structure (see figure 3.21). ICS consists of the following five areas of responsibility:

1. Operations
2. Logistics
3. Planning
4. Finance
5. Command

The number of people involved and the roles of each vary, depending upon the type and nature of the emergency. The duties and actions of each member of the ICS require specialized training, which is outside the scope of HAZWOPER.

Resources

Hundreds, perhaps thousands, of publications and reference documents containing information outlining the characteristics of hazardous substances are available from a variety of sources. Most, if not all, of the agencies discussed earlier have reference texts or databases available. Remember that no reference guide has a list of all of the hazardous materials known to man, and no guide has all the answers to your emergency or compliance needs. Some of the more helpful reference materials include the following:

- Material Safety Data Sheets (MSDSs)
- NIOSH Pocket Guide to Chemical Hazards (figure 3.22)
- Emergency Response Guidebook (ERG) (figure 3.23)
- Chemical Hazard Response Information System (CHRIS) CD-ROM

FIGURE 3.22
The NIOSH Pocket Guide to Chemical Hazards

Material Safety Data Sheets

MSDSs came about as a result of the Hazard Communication Standard, which was discussed earlier in this book. The standard requires all firms manufacturing and/or distributing chemicals for use in the United States to prepare MSDSs for those chemicals and distribute them to their customers (we are the customers).

The law further requires that employers provide their employees with an MSDS for every hazardous chemical that is present in the workplace. The MSDS is one of those items that is very functional, especially in the event of an emergency. It can actually save your life! The purpose of the MSDS is to inform you about the hazards associated with the chemical you might be working with at your next site. The law says that you must have access to the MSDS and be taught how to read and understand it (see figure 3.24).

The information that is printed on the MSDS is a summarization of the technical data from many sources. Training, knowledge, and understanding of this technical information will provide workers with the skills to safely deal with any occupational exposure that may arise. Each MSDS is different (even within the same manufacturing group), so it is necessary to take the time to read and understand it before you have to use it in an actual emergency situation. The MSDS tells workers the following:

FIGURE 3.23
The Emergency Response Guidebook

- Name of manufacturer/distributor, address, and phone
- 24-hour contact information
- Ingredients and physical properties of the materials
- Health hazards
- PPE needed for handling
- First-aid treatment if you become exposed
- How to handle an accidental spill or leak
- Fire fighting information
- Precautions for safe handling and use
- If the material is a carcinogen (cancer causing)

An understanding of how best to interpret the information from an MSDS is one of the best tools you can have. Knowing what information is on the sheet and where it's located is extremely helpful in an emergency. Remember that the format is different from MSDS to MSDS, so they are not all set up alike. If you encounter a material you are not sure about, read the

FIGURE 3.24
Material Safety Data Sheet

MSDS, and familiarize yourself and your coworkers with the information and precautions you may have to take.

An MSDS was once a two-page document. Now it is common to see an MSDS that is fifteen or more pages in length. They are only as good as the information that is provided to you. You have to use them to become familiar with the materials you'll encounter on the job. Don't wait until it's too late.

NIOSH Pocket Guide to Chemical Hazards

This book is helpful for identifying chemical and physical properties, PPE, and known health hazards for workers that work with hazardous materials. The hazardous substances are listed in the Chemical Listing section, in alphabetical order, four to a page. Other tables of codes and abbreviations to cross-reference, clarify, or expand information shown are shown in each chemical's listing. Tables of codes and the abbreviations are well-defined in the book. The information provided is very specific about each hazardous chemical listed.

Emergency Response Guidebook

The Emergency Response Guidebook (ERG) is published every three or four years by DOT. It is a "first-aid tool only," in my opinion. ERG is not going to solve the world's environmental problems; rather, it is designed to give guidance to people, such as facility managers, during the initial stages of a hazardous material emergency. Nothing in the book (for any of the more than 2,500 hazardous materials listed) is specific about any of the chemicals. Therefore, not everything you read in the book about the specific chemical you look up may be true! Although this may not give you a warm, fuzzy feeling, this won't get you into trouble, but instead will make you more cautious than you might have to be, considering the situation at hand.

Once you use this tool (ERG), I would recommend that a cross-comparison to another reference text or MSDS be used for more specific information. This reference book should not be used to determine compliance with the hazardous materials regulations or to develop safety plans for specific chemical situations. The reason I say that is because there is nothing specific in the book and the book is not designed for developing safety plans or determining compliance. This is an excellent reference text but is only one weapon in the arsenal, so to speak.

The Internet

With the invention of the Internet, a whole new world became available to facility managers with respect to environmental health and safety issues. The following are some web sites that you might find helpful:

- www.osha.gov
- www.epa.gov
- www.dot.gov
- www.maritime.edu
- www.fema.gov
- www.cdc.gov/niosh
- www.nfpa.org
- www.dhs.gov
- www.chrismanual.com

Summary

Regulations, the agencies that enforce them, and references are all key components in the effort to maintain compliance. Individuals working with hazardous materials and/or hazardous waste must have a professional, responsible, and mature attitude. The overall goal at the start of each work shift should be to take the necessary precaution to ensure that all employees in the facility return home safely. Using the OSHA standards and the reference texts described, as well as others that you or your company may have, will assist you in meeting this important daily goal. If you are not sure of the regulations or have a question regarding anything safety related, consult a safety professional.

4

Respiratory Protection Program

A NY EMPLOYER WHO REQUIRES OR PERMITS employees to wear a respirator must have a written respiratory protection program in place. This is required by OSHA in both the asbestos standard and the respiratory protection standard (29 CFR 1910.134). Some facility managers may have an ongoing asbestos abatement project or have asbestos issues in their facility. The written respirator program establishes some standard operating procedures concerning the use and maintenance of respiratory equipment. In addition to having such a written program, the employer must also be able to demonstrate that the program is effective, enforced, and updated as necessary. An annual review of the written program is required by OSHA to determine if your company is meeting these requirements.

Respiratory Program Requirements

The OSHA regulations spell out exactly what must be included in a written program. An effective respirator program should, at a minimum, include the following items:

- A written statement of company policy, including assignment of individual responsibility, accountability, and authority for required activities of the respiratory protection program
- Written standard operating procedures outlining the selection and use of respirators
- Respirator selection (from NIOSH-approved and -certified models) on the basis of hazards to which the worker may be exposed
- Medical examinations of workers to determine whether they may be assigned an activity where negative-pressure respiratory protection is required
- Employee training in the proper use and limitations of respirators (as well as a way to evaluate the skill and knowledge obtained by the worker through training)
- Respirator-fit testing (an annual requirement for all respirator wearers) (see figure 4.1)
- Regular cleaning and disinfecting of all respirators (recommended before and after every use) (see figure 4.2)
- Routine inspection of respirators during cleaning, and at least once a month and after each use for those respirators designated for emergency use only (see figure 4.3)

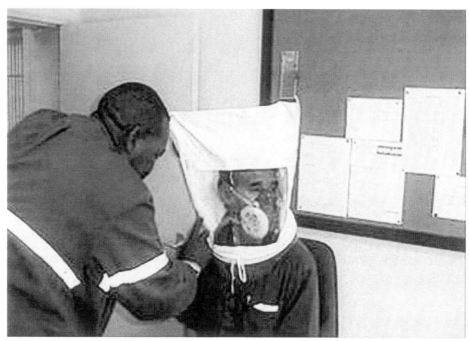

FIGURE 4.1
Respirator-fit testing

FIGURE 4.2
Respirator cleaning equipment

FIGURE 4.3
An authorized technician performing an inspection of respiratory equipment

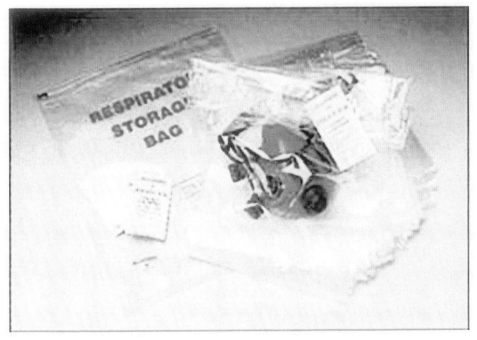

FIGURE 4.4
Proper respirator storage bags

- Storage of respirators in convenient, clean, and sanitary locations (not hung in the workplace or from a toolbox!) (see figure 4.4)
- Surveillance of work area conditions and the degree of employee exposure (e.g., through air monitoring)
- Regular inspection and evaluation of the continued effectiveness of the program (at least an annual review, but periodic evaluation is recommended)

All of the above items are required by OSHA if employees wear respirators during any work activities.

Keep in Mind

Respirators should be used for protection only when engineering controls have been shown to be infeasible for the control of the hazard or during the interim period when engineering controls are being set up or installed. Respiratory protection is a last resort, not the first line of defense for workers. If we can avoid having our personnel wear respirators, by all means we should attempt to do so. OSHA has determined that when personnel wear respirators:

- It takes longer to accomplish the task(s).
- It costs more to do the work.
- It is more taxing on the worker.

However, time to accomplish the work, regardless of the cost, or the toll it takes on the worker, if the respirator is needed to perform the work, it must be worn.

Establishing a Policy

Every employer needs to prepare a clear concise policy regarding the use of respirators by every employee who is required to wear one when performing any work requiring a respirator. This policy, at a minimum, should serve as the facility's guiding principal for the preparation, implementation, and enforcement of an effective respiratory protection program. The policy then needs to be shared with all of the workers who wear respirators, in an attempt to make them aware of what is expected from them and what the company policy is related to wearing, selecting the equipment, cleaning, storage, and review of the respirator program.

Designation of a Program Administrator

A program administrator must be designated by name. (Again, in many cases, this might be another duty for a facility manager.) This person is responsible for implementation of, and adherence to, the provisions of the respiratory protection program. It is usually a good idea to also designate a person who is responsible for enforcement of the procedures at each work area. Procedures should also be outlined for enforcement of the program. Enforcement procedures and the development of the program as a whole should be done in conjunction with and input from the employees who actually wear the respiratory protective equipment.

Selection and Use of Respiratory Protection Equipment

Respirators used must be selected from those approved by NIOSH for use in atmospheres requiring employees to don respirators. A NIOSH-approved respirator contains the following criteria:

- An assigned identification number associated with each respirator
- A label identifying the type of hazard the respirator is designed to protect against
- Additional information on the label that indicates limitations and identifies the component parts approved for use with the basic unit

Although some single-use disposable dust masks were at one time "approved" by NIOSH for use with asbestos, they should no longer be used during asbestos abatement projects. NIOSH has stated that these respirators do not provide adequate protection against asbestos fibers. As a rule of thumb, negative pressure, air-purifying respirators with high efficiency particulate (HEPA) filters may be used during asbestos abatement procedures.

Medical Approval

Only those individuals who are medically capable to wear respiratory protective equipment can be issued a respirator. Initially, before being issued one, an employee will need to receive applicable tests to evaluate his or her medical and physical conditions. The employee will be required

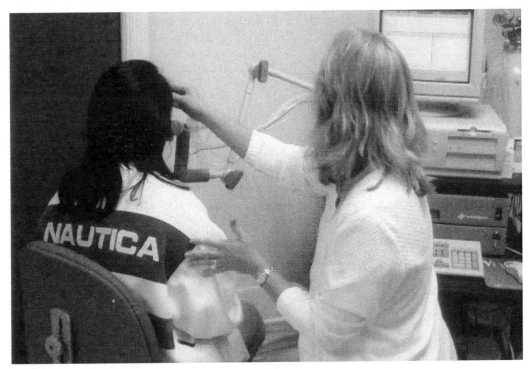

FIGURE 4.5
A spirometry test taking place

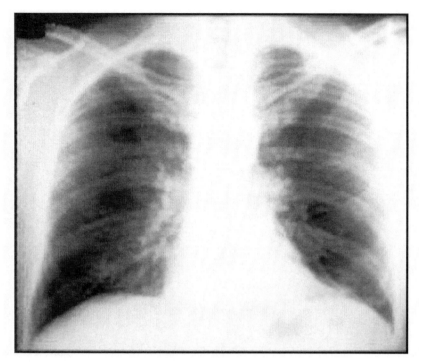

FIGURE 4.6
A chest X-ray

to be medically checked annually thereafter. Medical tests to be conducted by a physician often include the following:

- Pulmonary function test (such as spirometry) (see figure 4.5)
- A chest X-ray (if a physician or other licensed health care professional determines it is necessary) (see figure 4.6)
- Electrocardiogram (ECG) (see figure 4.7)
- Any other tests needed for proper evaluation by a physician

A medical history in the form of a questionnaire is collected for each individual. Other factors to be considered by a physician may include: emphysema, asthma, chronic bronchitis, heart disease, anemia, hemophilia, poor eyesight, poor hearing, hernia, lack of finger or hand usage, epileptic seizures, or other factors that might inhibit the ability of an employee to wear respiratory equipment.

Employee Training Program

Each employee designated to wear a respirator has to receive adequate training. The training session (initial and periodic training) should be conducted by a qualified individual to ensure that employees understand the limitations, use, and maintenance of respiratory equipment. Your facility may have a person on staff that can do this for you, or you may need to seek an outside source to conduct the training.

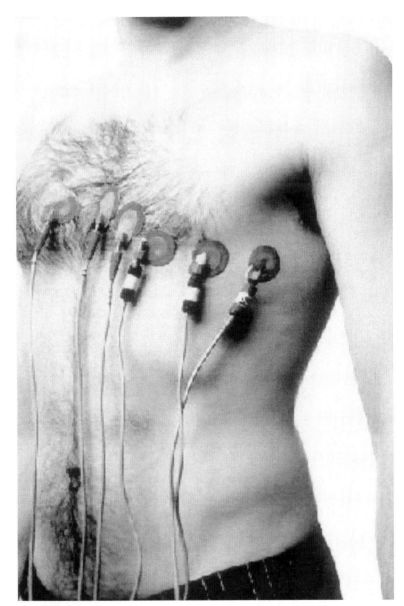

FIGURE 4.7
An employee having an ECG test

Respirator-Fit Testing

One of the most important elements of an effective respirator program is fit. The OSHA respirator standard (29 CFR 1910.134) requires that the fit of respirators be determined when the respirator is issued. I also like to check this every six months thereafter for all negative-pressure respirators. (The reason is that people gain or lose weight, their facial features may change, etc., and we want to ensure a proper fit for every facility worker wearing an air-purifying respirator.) Procedures for fit testing should be addressed in the facility's written respiratory program.

Cleaning and Disinfection of Respirators

Whenever possible, a respirator should be reserved for the exclusive use of a single facility worker. Following each use, the respirator should be cleaned and disinfected. The following procedures can be used to clean a respirator:

- Wash with a detergent or a detergent/disinfectant combination, in warm (not hot) water using a brush.
- Rinse in clean water, or rinse once with a disinfectant and once with clean water. The clean-water rinse is particularly important because traces of detergent or disinfectant left on the mask can cause skin irritation and/or damage some respirator components.
- Let the respirator air dry on a rack or hang; position the respirator so that the face piece rubber will not dry out of shape.

Inspection of the respirator is an important but routine task. It should be done before and after each use. The following items should be checked, at a minimum.

Routine Inspection of Respirators

1. Rubber face piece:
   - Dirt
   - Cracks, tears, or holes
   - Distortion from improper storage
   - Cracked, scratched, or loose-fitting lens
   - Broken or missing mounting clips
2. Headstraps:
   - Breaks or tears
   - Loss of elasticity
   - Broken or malfunctioning buckles or attachments
   - Excessively worn sections of the headstraps that might allow the face piece to slip
3. Valves
   - Detergent residue, dust, or dirt on the valve seat
   - Cracks, tears, or distortion in the valve
   - Missing or defective valve cover
4. Filter elements
   - Proper type of filter for the job and contaminants involved
   - Approved design
   - Missing or worn gaskets
   - Worn threads
   - Cracks or dents in the housing
   - Spent, dirty, used

Use of Respirators Is Least Satisfactory Method

Engineering controls and work practice controls are generally regarded as the most effective methods to control exposures to any airborne hazardous substances in the workplace. OSHA

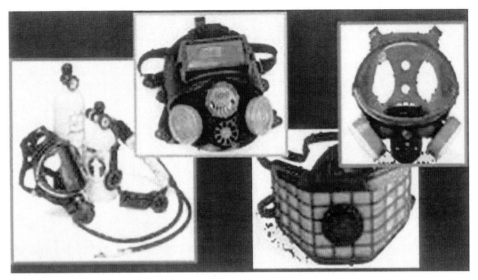

FIGURE 4.8
A variety of respirator types

considers the use of respirators to be the least satisfactory approach to exposure control because of the following reasons:

- Respirators provide adequate protection only if the employers ensure, on a continual basis, that they are properly fitted and worn correctly.
- Respirators protect only the employees who are wearing them from a hazard, rather than reducing or eliminating the hazard from the workplace as a whole (which is what engineering controls and work practice controls do).
- Respirators are uncomfortable to wear and cumbersome to use and interfere with communication in the workplace, which can sometimes be critical to maintaining safety and health.
- The costs of operating a functional respiratory protection program are substantial—including regular medical examinations, fit testing, training, and the purchasing of equipment (see figure 4.8).

So what does all of this mean? It means that if you don't have to wear a respirator—let's not wear it. On the other hand, if it is needed and you are unable to use engineering or administrative controls, then you and/or your employees must wear respiratory protection equipment.

Assigned Protection Factors for Respirators

New Assigned Protection Factors (APFs) for respiratory protection programs have recently been included into OSHA's respiratory protection standard.

This APF final rule completes the revision of the reserve sections of OSHA's Respiratory Protection Standard that were revised and published in 1998. The Respiratory Protection Standard now contains provisions needed for a comprehensive respiratory protection program, including selection and use of respirators, training, medical evaluation, and fit testing.

TABLE 4.1
Assigned Protection Factors for Various Types of Respirators

Respirator Class/Type	Assigned Protection Factor	
	OSHA	NIOSH
Air-Purifying		
Filtering Face piece	10	10
Half-Mask	10	10
Full Face piece	50	50
Powered Air-Purifying		
Half-Mask	50	50
Full Face piece	250	50
Loose-Fitting Face piece	25	25
Hood or Helmet	25	25
Supplied Air		
Half-Mask, Demand	10	10
Half-Mask, Continuous	50	50
Half-Mask, Pressure Demand	1,000	1,000
Full Face piece, Demand	50	50
Full Face piece, Continuous Flow	250	250
Full Face piece, Pressure Demand	1,000	1,000
Loose-Fitting Face-piece	25	25
Hood or Helmet	25	25
Self-Contained Breathing Apparatus		
Demand	50	50
Pressure Demand	>1,000	10,000

Assigned Protection Factors are numbers that indicate the level of workplace respiratory protection that a respirator or a certain class of respirators is expected to provide to employees when used as part of an effective respiratory protection program. An APF table is included in this section to guide employers in the selection of air-purifying, powered air-purifying, supplied-air (or airline respirator), and self-contained breathing apparatus (SCBA) respirators (table 4.1).

Employers must follow these new requirements and use APFs to select the appropriate type of respirator based upon the exposure limit of a specific contaminant and the level of the contaminant present in the workplace. Employers select respirators by comparing the exposure level found in the workplace and the maximum concentration of the contaminant in which a particular type of respirator can be used (the Maximum Use Concentration, or MUC). Employers generally determine the MUC by multiplying the respirator's APF by the contaminant's exposure limit. If the workplace level of the contaminant is expected to exceed the respirator's MUC, the employer must choose a respirator with a higher APF.

5

Site Security

IT SEEMS LIKE EVERY DAY, we read about some industry, school, facility, or complex having a lockdown, security breach, issue, or problem. Site access control is one of many challenges faced by facility managers, especially during construction or renovation projects. This is particularly difficult during renovation of occupied spaces. Effective controls require a great deal of preplanning and coordination of effort among the facility manager, contractors, project manager(s), and other departmental management involved in the process (see figure 5.1).

Especially after September 11, 2001, Americans are living with heightened fears due to increased threats of terrorism, yet many facilities have returned to the "old ways" with regard to security. Many facility managers, as the liaisons between upper management and the security contractors and vendors, are now faced with implementing new security procedures and policies.

Security should always be a top priority for facility managers, but in light of the September 11 terrorist attacks, managers must take a proactive role in also ensuring the safety of employees. Some tips for managers include the following:

- Stay alert to any local and international news/issues, which can change very rapidly and may affect your facility or industry in any way.
- Assess all areas of your facilities to determine potential risks and concerns. Be sensitive to your employees' concerns for their safety and being away from their loved ones in the event of a problem. Make changes as appropriate.
- Make security an integral part of all facility planning processes.
- Review your insurance policies to determine specific coverage for the types of issues that might face your facility.
- Review your facility travel policies and procedures to ensure that they address security threats and are relative to this ever-changing environment in which your facility now must operate.
- Ensure that emergency plans are integrated into daily activities. Develop a business continuity plan and contingency destinations and facilities in case an incident occurs.
- Establish a good working relationship with security management and know how they will support you and your facility, especially in the event of an incident.

FIGURE 5.1
A security booth at a facility

- Demand that contract and/or facility security personnel and companies are competent to protect your attendees and property.
- Develop an emergency plan that includes critical local resources that are available for your facility use. Maintain accurate lists of all current employees and their emergency contact information. Lists should be checked monthly to ensure that names and contact information are accurate.
- Provide employees with useful security, health, and safety guidelines.
- Brief the senior staff (and selected others) on the security and contingency plan and associated procedures.
- Establish effective access control policies and procedures for exclusive access by authorized personnel.
- If a crisis or emergency occurs, leadership and communication are key factors to the effective control and successful mitigation of the situation. Establish a single point of contact to avoid confusing or contradictory communications.
- Use only professional security resources that have an established track record and understand your facility's needs (see figure 5.2).

Facility Business Continuity Plan

Many chief executive officers (CEOs), business founders, or owners lost their lives in the September 11, 2001, attacks on the World Trade Center and Pentagon (and in the aircraft accidents

FIGURE 5.2
Professional security officers from Danner Company

associated with these two events), and many company operations were seriously damaged, some beyond recovery. It is clear that those with building and employee emergency organizations and business continuity plans survived more than those without plans (see figure 5.3).

I recommend that facility managers conduct a risk assessment of their business operations, office space, critical business elements, exterior environment, and so on to identify the various risks exposure. Facility managers should also develop and test a business continuity plan that includes emergency procedures and communications, a leadership succession plan for every key position in the company, current emergency contact information for all staff and key resources, and so on. Another suggestion is to automatically back up your company data daily and store it in a distinctly separate and secure location.

As a facility manager, it is wise to determine if your key suppliers, vendors, and contractors have business continuity plans (of their own) to continue supporting your business. If they do not have a business continuity plan, you should insist that they develop one or seek another contractor that can support your business, so that your facility can maintain its current operations with minimal disruptions.

Remember that our national and international economies depend upon each and every one of us vigilantly and attentively resuming business without fear.

Outsourcing

Immediately following the attacks of September 11, there was a sudden rush to strengthen and secure many of the country's commercial buildings. However, today facilities are making more

FIGURE 5.3
The business continuity cycle

balanced assessments and plans. Rather than using the quick-fix approach—visible security solutions that fail to address actual threats (which also are expensive)—a greater emphasis is being placed on threat assessments that lead to bona fide risk management.

For many facilities, applying translucent security, invisible to the public eye, is probably an appropriate solution to some of today's security issues. Facility managers might decide to implement transparent security wherever possible and avoid creating a jail-like look within the workplace or facility. They should carefully review design plans to maintain the integrity of the facility and its outbuildings and surrounding grounds, while trying to ensure facility safety. Company executives and facility managers should also agree on when and where the more visible security measures are appropriate.

Such levels of expertise are not always readily available for facility professionals within their own companies, so in order to develop and carry out meaningful security plans, many facilities have looked favorably at outsourcing these services (see figure 5.4).

Outsourced security consulting is a rapidly growing service sector. As with any dynamic market, several new companies and individuals have jumped on the bandwagon, in an attempt to take advantage of the high demand for this type of service/consulting need.

Problems with this rapidly increasing industry include the following:

- A lack of qualified providers
- Little or no industry standards
- A poorly educated consumer market (the facility sector)

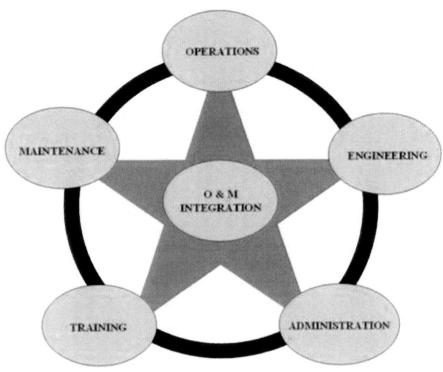

FIGURE 5.4
Outsourcing tips for facility managers

While exploring security companies, facility managers have to verify credentials through checking references and then determine the best options for their particular needs.

There are many organizations that offer security industry certifications. One of those organizations is ASIS International (American Society of Industrial Security) (see figure 5.5). This group qualifies security personnel with its Certified Protection Professional (CPP) and Physical Security Professional (PSP) programs.

FIGURE 5.5
The ASIS logo

FIGURE 5.6
Video security equipment

New Technology May Assist Managers

Video security and surveillance technologies have always been regarded as a deterrent measure. New technologies can now be linked with data integration to allow users to tie previously unrelated systems/areas together, making them more effective as a preventive tool (see figure 5.6). While information technology has made security systems more productive, it has also made them more complicated for the personnel to use.

It is my opinion that technology truly is a double-edged sword. While advancements in security equipment and surveillance technology have simplified many personal tasks and facility operations and increased efficiency, the repairs, modifications, and replacement of such technology devices have become so intricate that they frequently require professional technical expertise. Let's face it, the security industry is still adjusting to the new technologies and the transition from old VCRs to DVDs.

No Easy Solutions

Security solutions are not one-size-fits-all. Most of today's security installations are the result of a retrofit rather than new construction. Facility managers have to take into consideration what can and cannot be done based on local and statewide codes, ordinances, basic standards, guidelines, and the unique environments of their own facilities.

As with contract security services, technology is also being used to improve the efficiencies, productivity, and bottom-line return of physical security solutions as well. One perfect exam-

FIGURE 5.7
Key and access control equipment

ple of this trend is key and asset control. Key control represents not only a major concern for facility managers from a security/threat standpoint (i.e., unauthorized access, theft of property and equipment, etc.) but as a considerable cost issue and operating efficiency.

Key control and asset management systems have advanced from pegboards and paper sign-out sheets to electronically controlled, high-tech-based key lockers that release keys or other assets only to authorized individuals during approved time periods (see figure 5.7). These systems can generate real-time reports for facility managers and send out multiple alerts over a variety of mediums (Blackberry, pager, e-mail, PDA, cellular phone, to name a few) should keys go missing.

New physical security solutions require the cooperation of end users to be effective. Achieving buy-in from employees who will be working with the systems can be a major concern for facility managers. This is hard to accomplish in some places. Buy-in may be difficult, as employees may see this technology as "they don't trust us."

It is up to the facility manager to set the tone. Although employees may shy away at the difficulties associated with improving workplace security and safety, the people ultimately responsible for the site—facility managers—have to understand the threat is very real, and they must develop preventive and responsive measures to mitigate any risk to employees or the facility.

Many years after September 11, facilities are still wrestling with the security issues. Finding the correct balance to combat actual building threats instead of just throwing money at problems can be realized by doing a thorough assessment. Although it can be a major struggle (especially with all that managers have on their plates to deal with), adoption of manageable security measures is a practical goal for facility managers who understand innovation.

FIGURE 5.8
Access control at a facility

Site Access Control

When planning for site access control procedures, the following should be considered:

- Ensure that appropriate procedures are in place for controlling access to the facility during nonworking hours or anytime that the facility is unoccupied for any reason (e.g., lunch, breaks, weather, holidays, etc.) (see figure 5.8).
- Where entry into areas that are normally locked or otherwise normally closed to unauthorized personnel is required, ensure that documented steps are in place for the appropriate control over access to the space, that the area is locked whenever it is unoccupied, and that the area is checked, locked, and secured at the end of every workday (see figure 5.9).
- Ensure that areas "off limits" to nonauthorized personnel are clearly and appropriately posted (see figure 5.10).
- Where facility activities require closing of exits or egress routes (with the approval of city or town building and/or fire officials), ensure the affected exit signs are covered to prevent confusion and that alternate routes are clearly posted. Notices should be given to personnel in advance, if at all possible, to advise them of these situations (see figure 5.11).
- Ensure that the appropriate employees or security contractors understand their responsibilities to require any unauthorized personnel to leave the facility and surrounding areas immediately and to report these incidents to the company's facility manager and, if necessary, to the security department, if your company has one. If your facility doesn't have a security department, perhaps the police should be contacted in these situations.
- The use of barricades and signs is an important part of any facility (see figure 5.12). Barricades should act as physical barriers, preventing contact by passersby (including coworkers)

FIGURE 5.9
Lack of security (open gate)

FIGURE 5.10
Access sign

No access
to
construction
traffic

FIGURE 5.11
Closure sign

with the hazards created by construction or certain maintenance activities, while signs should be used to direct traffic, both vehicular and pedestrian, safely through or around the work area or facility.

Signage Tips

While barricades and signs should be used wherever necessary for the physical protection of people or the facility, the following is only a partial list of activities where their use is required by various codes or regulations:

FIGURE 5.12
Security barriers at work

FIGURE 5.13
Construction debris chute

- Wherever any construction debris is dropped without the use of an enclosed chute (see figure 5.13)
- Any areas that have temporary wiring operating at more than 600 volts
- Work areas in the facility for electrical equipment with exposed and/or energized parts
- The swing radius of the rotating superstructure of cranes or other pieces of heavy construction-related equipment (see figure 5.14)
- Wherever heavy equipment or vehicles are left unattended near a roadway at night (see figure 5.15)
- Trenching and/or excavations (need to be covered at shift end or filled in)
- Areas used for the preparation of explosive charges or any area for blasting operations (see figure 5.16)
- Street openings, such as manholes and sewers.
- Construction areas in energized electrical substations

FIGURE 5.14
A crane operating at a site

FIGURE 5.15
Unattended equipment left in road at night

FIGURE 5.16
Workers prepare for setting an explosive charge

New Regulations to Secure Certain High-Risk Facilities

As previously mentioned, as a consequence of September 11, 2001, security has become a vital issue at many facilities. The President of the United States recommended the establishment of the Department of Homeland Security (DHS) and Congress authorized it. While many of your facilities do not fall under the auspices of the DHS, many do (see figure 5.17). Even if DHS does not oversee your facility, it benefits all of us to step up the security efforts. DHS has made, available for public review, an aggressive and comprehensive set of proposed regulations that will improve security at high-risk chemical facilities across the nation.

The regulations will require that chemical facilities fitting certain profiles complete a secure online risk assessment to assist in determining their overall level of risk. High-risk facilities will then be required to conduct vulnerability assessments and submit site security plans that meet the department's performance standards. DHS will validate all submissions through audits and, in some cases, site inspections, and will also provide technical assistance to facility

FIGURE 5.17
DHS logo

owners and operators as needed. Performance standards will be designed to achieve specific outcomes, such as:

- Securing the perimeter of the facility and some critical targets (see figure 5.18)
- Controlling access
- Deterring theft of potentially dangerous chemicals
- Preventing internal sabotage

FIGURE 5.18
A chemical facility

Security strategies needed to satisfy these strict standards will depend upon the level of risk at each facility.

The proposed regulations provide chemical facilities with two quick and simple opportunities to challenge the disapproval of a site security plan. Failure to comply with performance standards could result in civil penalties up to $25,000 per day, and egregious instances of noncompliance could result in an order to cease facility operations.

Since 2003, DHS has worked closely with the chemical industry as well as state and local authorities on strengthening security at chemical facilities throughout the country. Most chemical facilities have already initiated voluntary security programs and made significant investments to achieve satisfactory security levels for their facilities. The Homeland Security Appropriations Act of 2007 granted DHS authority to regulate the security of high-risk chemical facilities. The proposed regulations contemplate immediate implementation at the highest of risk facilities, and a phased implementation at other chemical facilities that present security risks addressed by the statute.

6

The Environmental Management System

A NOTHER IMPORTANT PART OF MANY COMPANY OPERATIONS is environmental management. The Environmental Management System (EMS) is a process used to support various facilities in their ongoing effort to incorporate environmental concerns into their daily operational practices. An EMS offers methods for the development of policies and procedures, awareness and training, internal and external communication, planning means for continual improvement, and performance measurement. The EMS contains methods for regulatory tracking and regulatory relationships, auditing functions, environmental management information systems, risk management, budgeting, accounting, record-keeping, and documentation. An EMS includes pollution prevention, sustainability efforts, green-building efforts, and compliance with all applicable local, state, and federal laws and regulations. At many companies, the facility manager is responsible for implementation of environmental health and safety programs designed to ensure regulatory compliance with safety and environmental regulations and coordinate the overall company EMS and compliance effort, perhaps with the help of other company departments and groups.

The facility manager is required to implement a number of environmental compliance programs to comply with EPA requirements. An effective EMS attempts to tie together various features of the company's efforts into an integrated program and compliance approach to environmental protection.

International Organization for Standardization
14000 Series Environmental Management Systems

International Organization for Standardization (ISO) 14000, ISO 14001, ISO 14004, and so forth—the myriad of ISO 14000 standards and information related to environmental management can sometimes hinder progress and cause mass confusion. What do all of those numbers mean, you might ask (see figure 6.1). This chapter is designed to attempt to simplify these—to make environmental management, using the above standards, a much easier task for the facility manager.

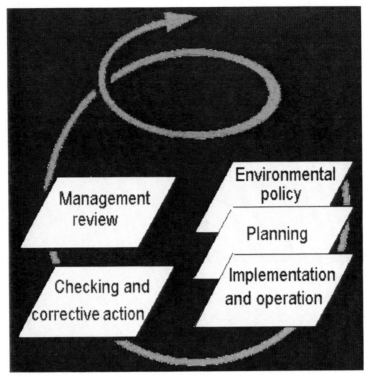

FIGURE 6.1
ISO 14000 information

I will attempt to explain each of these standards and items and identify a series of simple-to-use resources and guides that are available. Hopefully, this will help to ensure that you (and your company) meet your obligations diligently and professionally, with a minimum of problems.

What Is ISO 14000?

ISO 14000 is a series of international standards on environmental management. It provides a guideline for the development of an environmental management system and the supporting audit program that accompanies it. The main focus for its development came as a result of the Rio Summit on the Environment, held in 1992.

History of ISO 14000

As a number of national standards emerged (British Standard BS 7750 being the first), ISO created a group to investigate how such standards might be of some benefit to the business and industry communities. As a result, this group made a recommendation that an ISO committee be initiated to create an international standard.

If there were no standards, we would soon notice. Standards make an enormous contribution to most aspects of our lives—although very often, that contribution is invisible. It is when there is an absence of standards that their importance is brought home. For example, as purchasers or users of products, we soon notice when they turn out to be of poor quality, do not fit, are incompatible with equipment we already have, or are unreliable, unsafe, or dangerous. When products meet our expectations, we tend to take this for granted. We are usually unaware of the role played by standards in raising levels of quality, safety, reliability, efficiency, and interchangeability—and in providing such benefits at an economical cost.

ISO is the world's largest developer of standards. Although ISO's principal activity is the development of technical standards, ISO standards also have important economic and social repercussions. ISO standards make a positive difference, not just to engineers and manufacturers for whom they solve basic problems in production and distribution but to society as a whole.

The international standards that ISO develops are very useful. They are useful to industrial and business organizations of all types, to governments and other regulatory bodies, to trade officials, to conformity assessment professionals, to suppliers and customers of products and services in both public and private sectors, and, ultimately, to people in general in their roles as consumers and end users.

ISO standards contribute to making the development, manufacturing, and supply of products and services more efficient, safer, and cleaner. They make trade between countries easier and fairer. They provide governments with a technical base for health, safety, and environmental legislation. They aid in transferring technology to developing countries. ISO standards also serve to safeguard consumers and users in general of products and services—as well as to make their lives simpler.

What Makes ISO 9000 and ISO 14000 So Special

The ISO 9000 and ISO 14000 families are among ISO's most widely known standards. ISO 9000 has become an international reference for quality requirements in most business-to-business dealings, and ISO 14000 looks set to achieve at least as much, if not more, in helping organizations to meet their ever-changing environmental challenges.

The vast majority of ISO standards are highly specific to a particular product, material, or process. However, the standards that have earned the ISO 9000 and ISO 14000 families a worldwide reputation are known as "generic management system standards." The word *generic* means that the same standards can be applied to any organization (facility), large or small, whatever its product—including whether its "product" is actually a service—in any sector of activity and whether it is a business enterprise, a public administration, or a government department. The "management system" refers to what the organization does to manage its processes, or activities. "Generic" also signifies that no matter what the facility is or does, if it wants to establish a quality management system or an environmental management system, then such a system has a number of essential features that are spelled out in the relevant standards of the ISO 9000 or ISO 14000 documents.

ISO 9000 is concerned with "quality management." This is what the facility does to enhance customer satisfaction by meeting customer and applicable regulatory requirements and continually striving to improve its performance in this regard. ISO 14000 is primarily concerned with "environmental management," which is what the facility does to minimize any harmful effects on the environment caused by its activities and how it continually attempts to improve its environmental performance.

Conformity Assessment Is Important

At its simplest, "conformity assessment" means checking that products, materials, services, systems, or people measure up to the specifications of a relevant standard. In today's society, many products require testing for conformance with a variety of specifications or for compliance with safety or other regulations before they can be put on many markets. Even simpler products may require supporting technical documentation that includes test data. With so much trade taking place across borders, conformity assessment has become an important component of the world economy. Over the years, ISO has developed many of the standards against which products are assessed for conformity, as well as the standardized test methods that allow the meaningful comparison of test results so necessary for international trade. ISO itself does not carry out conformity assessment. However, in partnership with IEC (International Electrotechnical Commission), ISO develops ISO/IEC guides and standards to be used by organizations that carry out conformity assessment activities. The voluntary criteria contained in these guides and standards represent an international consensus on what constitutes best practices. Their use

FIGURE 6.2
ISO 14001 certificate

contributes to the consistency and coherence of conformity assessment worldwide and thus facilitates trade across borders.

What Is ISO 14001?

The ISO 14001 document is the cornerstone standard of the entire ISO 14000 series. It specifies a structure of control for an EMS against which an organization can be certified by a third party (see figure 6.2).

Other ISO14000 Series Standards

Other standards in the series are actually guidelines. Many of these guidelines were written to help you—the facility manager—achieve registration to ISO 14001. These documents include the following:

- ISO 14004 provides guidance on the development and implementation of EMSs
- ISO 14010 provides general principles of environmental auditing (now superseded by ISO 19011)
- ISO 14011 provides specific guidance on auditing an EMS (now superseded by ISO 19011)
- ISO 14012 provides guidance on qualification criteria for environmental auditors and lead auditors (now superseded by ISO 19011)
- ISO 14013/5 provides audit program review and assessment material
- ISO 14020+ details labeling issues
- ISO 14030+ provides guidance on performance targets and monitoring within an EMS
- ISO 14040+ covers life cycle issues

Of all these, ISO 14001 is not only the most well-known but is the only ISO 14000 standard against which it is currently possible to be certified by an external certification authority.

Obtaining ISO certification is a rather lengthy process and involves a great deal of teamwork and preparation. Once the certification is received, your facility needs to maintain it—an even harder task!

7

Hazardous Waste Management

FACILITY MANAGERS OFTEN FIND THEMSELVES RESPONSIBLE for dealing with hazardous materials and the hazardous waste at their companies. Hazardous waste may be generated from a variety of facility operations, including:

- Laboratory operations
- Maintenance
- Construction projects
- Renovation activities
- Photo processing
- A variety of other activities at any facility

Hazardous waste is a particular class of "solid" waste (that includes solid, liquid, or gaseous material), which, if improperly managed, poses a substantial threat or potential hazard to human health and the environment (see figure 7.1). Hazardous waste is also different from hazardous materials. We could not operate in our daily lives without hazardous materials. Think about all of the cleaning products used at work or home. Look under your sink or in the garage for even more hazardous materials. So when does a hazardous material become a hazardous waste?

- When the material is not used properly
- When the material is not stored properly
- When the material is not transported properly
- When the material is spent or used up

Typical hazardous wastes generated at some facilities include, but are not limited to:

- Spent acids and solvents
- Other used chemicals
- Waste paints
- Waste oil

FIGURE 7.1
Hazardous waste management operations at a facility

The handling and storage of hazardous waste is subject to very strict specific regulations to ensure that uniform and consistent waste identification, storage, and disposal procedures are followed by personnel trained in the proper management of these wastes. There is also a great deal of liability for facilities for noncompliance. Compliance is a responsibility that cannot be reassigned to others. The EPA assigns the generator of hazardous waste "cradle-to-grave" responsibility for the proper management of these substances once generated (see figure 7.2). (All generators are issued their own generator identification number.) This stringent liability creates a powerful incentive for regulatory compliance, including waste minimization. In most states, there is a Department of Environmental Protection (DEP), or similarly titled entity, that is responsible for the implementation and enforcement of hazardous waste regulations. Enforcement is primarily conducted through unannounced site inspections, although there are other methods of enforcement used.

Oftentimes, the facility manager has sole responsibility or is responsible for assisting company personnel with hazardous waste management procedures, including waste identification, storage, packaging, manifesting, shipping, disposal, reporting, record-keeping, and personnel

FIGURE 7.2
Cradle-to-grave cycle

training. This responsibility carries with it a great deal of work, depending on the amount of hazardous waste that the company generates. This chapter provides facility managers involved in the management of hazardous waste with an overview of regulatory requirements for the management of these wastes. EPA 40 CFR and your state regulations are two resources you should have available for reference, if you have any responsibility for hazardous waste management at your facility.

Summary of Requirements

The scope and complexity of regulatory requirements that waste generators are subject to is directly related to a generator's "status." A generator's status is based on the quantity of hazardous waste generated per facility on a monthly basis. Being from Massachusetts (MA), I will use that state's information, but generally the status of generators is similar. You should refer to your state's regulations for additional information. The MA DEP has established specific hazardous waste regulations for large-quantity generators (LQG), small-quantity generators (SQG), and very small-quantity generators (VSQG) (see figure 7.3). DEP has assigned a separate status for the generation of waste oil (some states do the same thing).

The following summary provides a general overview of regulatory requirements applicable to most generators of hazardous waste.

1. Waste Identification: Hazardous waste includes substances that are solids, liquids, and gases (see figure 7.4). The EPA definition of hazardous waste includes substances that possess a hazardous characteristic (e.g., toxic, ignitable, corrosive, or reactive with other

FIGURE 7.3
A small-quantity generator

FIGURE 7.4
Worker writing EPA ID numbers on drum labels

FIGURE 7.5
Hazardous waste label

substances) or substances that are listed as hazardous waste by the EPA on the basis of their usage or chemical constituents.

2. Labeling: Containers that store hazardous waste must be properly and clearly labeled (see figure 7.5). Labels must include: (1) the words "Hazardous Waste," (2) the container contents in words (e.g., "WASTE OIL"), (3) the hazards associated with the waste in words (e.g., "TOXIC"), and (4) the accumulation start date. Once a satellite accumulation container becomes filled or otherwise ready for removal, the accumulation start date must be written on the label of the container.

3. Accumulation and Storage: Hazardous waste regulations establish a two-tiered waste accumulation and storage system: satellite accumulation and main accumulation (see figure 7.6).

• Satellite Accumulation: Hazardous waste accumulation and storage that is at the point of generation and under the control of the person generating the waste is called satellite accumulation. Regulations allow a maximum of 55 gallons of hazardous waste or one quart of acutely hazardous waste at each satellite accumulation area. Satellite accumulation containers must be closed unless waste is being added or removed from the container. Full containers of hazardous waste may be stored at the point of generation for a maximum of three days before being transferred to a designated, main accumulation area that has certain design and monitoring requirements (see figure 7.7).

• Main Accumulation: Main accumulation and storage of hazardous waste is subject to strict time limitations. Large-quantity generators of hazardous waste are allowed to store hazardous waste onsite for a maximum of 90 days.

FIGURE 7.6
A hazardous waste accumulation area

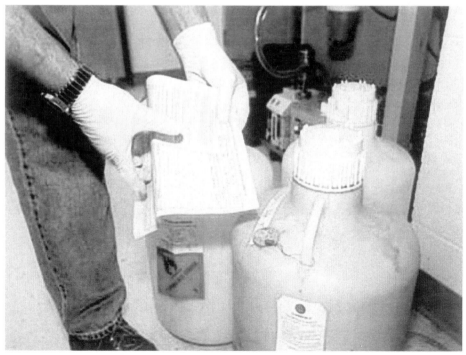

FIGURE 7.7
Satellite accumulation area materials being moved to hazardous waste area

FIGURE 7.8
A licensed hazardous waste transporter pumping at a facility

4. Manifesting: Hazardous waste must be shipped with a special shipping paper called a hazardous waste manifest. Manifest copies are to be retained in facility files for at least three years.
5. Transportation and Disposal: Hazardous waste must be transported only by a licensed hazardous waste transporter and can be sent only to a licensed treatment, storage, and disposal facility (TSDF) (see figure 7.8).
6. Emergency Preparedness and Prevention: In accordance with regulatory requirements, most facilities maintain a Hazardous Waste Management Contingency Plan. This plan is designed to prevent and to minimize hazards to public health, safety, or welfare or the environment from fires, explosions, spills, or other unplanned releases of hazardous waste. Hazardous waste regulations also require generators to comply with emergency preparedness and prevention requirements. These requirements include a testing and maintenance program for various emergency equipment (e.g., fire and spill equipment, emergency alarms, and communication systems) and the posting of a written up-to-date call list at the nearest telephone in an area where hazardous waste is managed. The list should include the following:

   • Names of emergency coordinators and contact information
   • The locations of emergency, fire, and spill-related equipment
   • Emergency telephone numbers of fire, police, and so on.
   • Evacuation routes, where applicable

   Hazardous waste generators are required to make arrangements with local emergency agencies, such as the fire department, police department, spill response contractors, and state and local emergency planning committees.
7. Waste Minimization: Generators of hazardous waste are required by the EPA to minimize the volume and toxicity of the hazardous waste they generate.
8. Recycling: Hazardous waste recycling activities require a permit. Facility managers should contact a consultant or their licensed hazardous waste contractor for assistance with permitting requirements if they intend to conduct hazardous waste recycling.

FIGURE 7.9
Facility managers at annual training

Training

Personnel involved in the management of hazardous waste must complete a training program that teaches them how to perform their duties in compliance with applicable hazardous waste regulations. Persons must be trained within six months of being hired and annually thereafter. Generators are required to maintain a written training program that describes training program contents, who is trained and why, and record-keeping procedures. Initial training should consist of a classroom training session. Thereafter, annual refresher training can be conducted in the classroom or by a web-based, online hazardous waste training program or another appropriate method of training (see figure 7.9).

Reporting

Some of the typical reporting requirements for generators of hazardous waste are as follows:

- Generators are required to submit a biennial hazardous waste report that summarizes hazardous waste generation and management activity for the previous year (generally a state requirement).
- Copies of hazardous waste manifests generally must be submitted to the DEP within 10 days.
- Any change in generation status or types of hazardous waste generated requires prompt notification to the state regulatory authority.

These reporting requirements must be assigned to an individual so that compliance is maintained.

FIGURE 7.10
An inspector conducting a walkthrough of a facility

Inspections

Regulations require that hazardous waste areas (satellite and main accumulation areas) be inspected on a weekly basis. Oftentimes, personnel utilizing a satellite accumulation are responsible for conducting this inspection. A weekly inspection checklist is provided in appendix B. Inspections must be conducted weekly and the reports or checklists maintained for at least three years (see figure 7.10).

Record-keeping

Hazardous waste regulations require that the following records be maintained for a minimum of three years:

- Waste analysis/determination records
- Manifests
- Biennial reports
- Exception reports

Land disposal restriction (LDR) notifications/certifications that typically accompany hazardous waste manifests are required to be maintained for a minimum of five years. Manifest and

LDR notifications/certifications copies should be forwarded to the EHS department, if your facility has one, or maintained by the facility manager, for retention and compilation into an EPA-required biennial report of facility waste activities. Exception reports are required to be filed with the DEP if and when certain copies of hazardous waste manifests are not received by specified time limits. Check the state requirements for further information on exception reports.

8

Hazardous Waste Training

A S DISCUSSED EARLIER IN CHAPTER 7 (Hazardous Waste Management), compliance is not an option or a suggestion, it is a requirement. Some facility managers may not be sure if their employees need training. Here are some guidelines that may be able to answer some of the most frequently asked questions about the EPA's hazardous waste training standard.

If you are shipping hazardous waste or other hazardous materials, you may be subject to DOT's training mandate.

1. Generators must train their personnel.

Any generator accumulating waste onsite is required to train its personnel. This requirement is part of the "accumulation rules" at 40 CFR 262.34.

Large-quantity generators (those who generate > 1,000 kg (2,200 lbs) total of all hazardous waste in any given month) are regulated under Section 262.34(a). Such generators are subject to the same training standard as TSDFs. In fact, Section 262.34(a)(4) refers generators to TSDF training rules at 40 CFR 265.16. This rule requires specific training, according to a written, site-specific training plan and requires written records of all training given.

"Small-quantity generators" (those who generate 100–1,000 kg [220-2,200 lbs] total of all hazardous waste in any given month) are not subject to the detailed requirements of Section 265.16, but they are still required to "ensure that all employees are thoroughly familiar with proper waste handling and emergency procedures relevant to their responsibilities" according to 40 CFR 262.34(d)(5)(iii). If a small-quantity generator exceeds the threshold and becomes a large-quantity generator in any given month, it must comply with large-quantity generators' rules immediately. If you believe that your facility is likely to become a large-quantity generator, all aspects of compliance, including the written training plan, should be in place and ready.

2. Who needs to be trained?

Under 40 CFR 265.16, generators must have records of appropriate training for all "facility personnel." This includes "all persons who work at, or oversee the operations of, a hazardous waste facility and whose actions or failure to act may result in noncompliance . . . ," according to the definition at 40 CFR 260.10. It should be noted that this definition is not limited to actual full-time employees, but may include part-time or temporary workers, contractors, consultants, and others at your facility. It may also include any and all offsite managers.

3. What training is required for your personnel?

   The EPA provides two performance standards:

   - All facility personnel must be taught ". . . to perform their duties in a way that ensures the facility's compliance with . . ." applicable regulations at 40 CFR 265.16(a)(2).
   - The training ". . . must include instruction which teaches . . . waste management procedures . . . relevant to the positions in which they are employed," as per 40 CFR 265.16(a)(2).

The details on how your facility intends to accomplish these objectives must be documented in a formal written hazardous waste training plan. Ultimately, the training must ensure that each person is performing his or her duties correctly (i.e., no violations are occurring). If a violation or problem occurs, it is an indication of insufficient training and refresher training must be provided.

4. Isn't this training just for emergency response personnel?

   There is an unfortunate misunderstanding that has arisen from the way in which EPA training requirements are written. The training rule emphasizes that training must include training on the facility's hazardous waste contingency plan and on specific emergency response procedures (see figure 8.1). These details are in addition to the general performance standards described previously.

FIGURE 8.1
Emergency responders at a training exercise

5. How much training is required (40 hours, 24 hours, etc.)?

Unlike OSHA, the EPA does not specify a particular duration of training. Again, this is left to site-by-site determination by the facility management, based on site-specific needs.

6. How often is training required?

EPA specifies at 40 CFR 265.16(c) that personnel ". . . must take part in an annual review of the initial training required. . . ." Again, particulars as to how detailed the annual retraining must be are left to the discretion of the individual facility manager. Some training may be appropriate to repeat in its entirety. Other training may require only a brief overview.

7. What if I hire a contractor to manage my hazardous wastes?

EPA requires hazardous waste generators to have a written training plan and training records for all personnel. This includes contractor employees. If you rely on contractors to assist in onsite waste management, their training must be included in your written training plan.

The rules provide that new personnel may work under the direct supervision of a trained person for up to six months. If you have occasional one-time contractors onsite for less than six months, you may satisfy their training requirements by ensuring that they are supervised in all hazardous waste management–related aspects of their jobs.

8. How does EPA training relate to training required by OSHA or DOT?

DOT also requires training for persons shipping or transporting hazardous materials (including hazardous wastes) according to 49 CFR 172.700.

Two of the most common OSHA chemical hazard training standards include:

- The Hazard Communication Standard (sometimes referred to as "employees' right-to-know") requires general workplace chemical hazard training, as well as chemical labeling and MSDSs in accordance with 29 CFR 1910.1200.
- The Hazardous Waste Operations Standard (HAZWOPER) requires specific training for persons involved in hazardous waste site cleanup, permitted TSDF operations, or emergency response to hazardous material spills, leaks, or releases outside their ordinary workplace, as per 29 CFR 1910.120.

EPA, DOT, and OSHA requirements are distinct and separate. It is generally good management practice to combine training into a single session where regulatory agency requirements are similar; however, facility managers have to ensure that they comply with each rule individually.

9. Important Regulatory References on Training

- 40 CRF 262.34(a)(4): Rule for large-quantity generators to comply with TSDF training rules at 40 CFR 265.16
- 40 CFR 264.16 and 265.16: Detailed standards for "personnel" training and for planning and documenting such training
- 40 CFR 260.10: Definition of "personnel"
- 45 FR (Final Rule) 72026, October 30, 1980: EPA discussion of the definition of "personnel" and its applicability to contractors and other non-employees

9

Asbestos

ASBESTOS WAS INCORPORATED INTO A NUMBER of widely used products, many of which were used in building construction beginning in the late 1800s. By the mid-1980s, most products containing asbestos were removed from the market. As facility managers, we now must deal with the various regulatory requirements that have been instituted over the years. The most common use of asbestos in many facilities was in floor tiles, mastic, thermal systems insulation (TSI), ceiling tiles, structural steel fireproofing, and acoustical and decorative plaster (see figure 9.1).

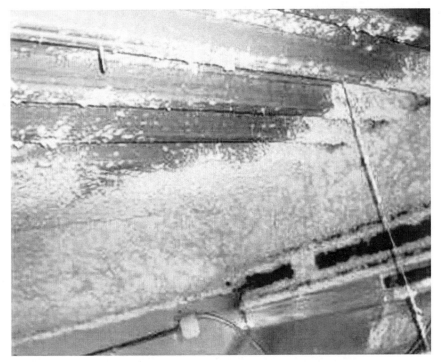

FIGURE 9.1
Asbestos on structural components used as fireproofing material

TABLE 9.1
Examples of Products That May Contain Asbestos

Subdivision	Generic Name	Asbestos (%)	Dates of Use	Binder/Sizing
Friable insulation material	Spray-applied Insulation	1–95	1935–1970	Sodium silicate, portland cement, organic binders
Preformed thermal insulating products	Batts, blocks, and pipe covering	15, 6–8	1926–1949	Magnesium carbonate
	85% magnesia calcium silicate		1949–1971	Calcium silicate
Textiles	Cloth fire blankets	100	1910–1980	None
	Felts:			
	Blue stripe	90–95	1910–1980	Cotton/wool
	Red stripe	80	1910–1980	
	Green stripe	90	1910–1980	
	Sheets	50–95	1920–1980	Cotton/wool
	Cord, rope, yarn	80–100	1920–1980	Cotton/wool
	Tubing	80–85	1920–1980	Cotton/wool
	Tape/strip	80–85	1920–1980	Cotton/wool
	Curtains (theater, welding)	60–65	1945–1980	Cotton
Cementitious concrete–like products	Extrusion panels:	8	1965–1977	Portland cement
	Corrugated	20–45	1930–1980	
	Flat	40–50	1930–1980	
	Flexible	30–50	1930–1980	
	Flexible perforated	30–50	1930–1980	
	Laminated	35–50	1930–1980	
	Roof tiles	20–30	1930–1980	
	Clapboard and shingles:			
	Clapboard	12–15	1944–1945	Portland cement
	Siding shingles	12–14	unknown–1980	
	Roofing shingles	20–32	unknown–1980	
	Pipe	20–15	1935–1980	Portland cement
Paper products	Corrugated:			
	High temperature	90, 35–70	1935–1980	Sodium silicate
	Moderate temperature		1910–1980	Starch
	Indented	98	1935–1980	Cotton and organic
	Millboard	80–85	1925–1980	Starch, lime, clay
Roofing felts	Smooth surface	10–15	1910–1980	Asphalt
	Mineral surface	10–15	1910–1980	Asphalt
	Shingles	1	1971–1974	Asphalt
	Pipeline	10	1920–1980	Asphalt
Compounds	Caulking putties	20	1930–1980	Linseed oil
	Adhesive (cold-applied)	5–25	1945–1980	Asphalt

Subdivision	Generic Name	Asbestos (%)	Dates of Use	Binder/Sizing
	Joint compound		1945–1975	Asphalt
	Roofing asphalt	5	Unknown–1980	Asphalt
	Mastics	5–25	1920–1980	Asphalt
	Asphalt tile cement	13–25	1959–1980	Asphalt
	Roof putty	10–25	Unknown–1980	Asphalt
	Plaster/stucco	2–10	Unknown–1980	Portland cement
	Spackles	3–5	1930–1975	Starch, casein
	Sealants (fire/water)	50–55	Sealants (fire/water)	Castor oil or polyisobutylene
	Cement, insulation	20–100	1900–1973	Clay
	Cement, finishing	55	1920–1973	Clay
	Cement, magnesia	15	1926–1950	Magnesium carbonate
Asbestos ebony products		50	1926–1950	Portland cement
Floor tile and sheet goods	Vinyl/asbestos floor tile	21, 26–33	1950–1980	Polyvinylchloride
	Asphalt/asbestos		1920–1980	Asphalt
	Sheet goods, resilient	30	1950–1980	Dry oils
Wall covering	Vinyl wallpaper	6–8	Unknown–1980	—
Paints and coatings	Roof coating	4–7	1900–1980	Asphalt
	Airtight	15	1940–1980	Asphalt

Asbestos abatement is regulated by OSHA. Abatement activities taken in facilities are also regulated by your particular state's DEP.

Per the OSHA Asbestos Standard (29 CFR 1926.1101), building materials installed prior to 1980 must be presumed to contain asbestos unless historical information or testing indicates otherwise. A list of products that might contain asbestos is included in table 9.1.

Prior to any facility maintenance or renovation projects, the facility manager should be responsible for arranging a survey to determine if asbestos-containing building material is present in the work area and, if so, whether it will be impacted by the planned work. Larger-scale projects may require an outside firm to test and design abatement.

Structures built prior to 1981 may have asbestos warning notices on the back of mechanical room doors. The notices may consist of an initial warning that the building may contain asbestos-containing materials (ACM), a list of products that may contain asbestos, and a notice that lists the results of previous sampling performed in the space (see figure 9.2).

Asbestos does not always need to be removed if it will not be disturbed. In some cases, management in-place may be advisable. If abatement is needed, some state regulations require submission and approval of an asbestos abatement design, use of a state-licensed firm to perform the abatement, air monitoring at the perimeter of the abatement area during removal

FIGURE 9.2
Label that shows asbestos-containing materials

and inspection, and clearance testing of the abated area prior to re-occupancy. In most cases, an outside contractor performs each of these functions (see figure 9.3).

Under no circumstances shall facility or contracted workers damage or disturb known or suspect ACM unless they are a licensed asbestos abatement contractor and have been specifically employed to perform asbestos repair or removal.

If suspect asbestos materials are discovered during the course of any work, the facility manager should suspend work that could disturb the material and contact the appropriate person/agency for testing of the materials.

FIGURE 9.3
An asbestos contractor at work

FIGURE 9.4
Sign advising workers of asbestos dangers

The facility manager should ensure employees and contractors are informed of the location of suspect and known ACM and that materials that might be impacted by the work have been abated (see figure 9.4). ACM must be disposed in a secure landfill in a manner consistent with relevant state and federal regulations. It cannot be disposed of in regular household trash.

Some projects may indirectly disturb ACM. For example, where asbestos is sprayed on the structural beam above the ceiling tiles, small amounts of ACM may loosen and fall onto the surface of the ceiling tile. To avoid personal exposure or building contamination, a licensed asbestos abatement contractor must be hired to clean the surface of the ceiling tiles before they are removed or displaced.

10

Safety Meetings

GOOD INTERNAL COMMUNICATION IS NECESSARY to relay important information up and down the chain of command in any facility. There are, obviously, many ways to accomplish effective communication, but one way is the safety meeting. It is a way of informing personnel of safety-related topics, and it serves as a reminder in some cases, but in other cases, it's a real awareness for employees. Also, here's a reminder to facility managers: No job is ever complete until the paperwork is done. Having said that, it is imperative that the safety meetings be documented and the records maintained. If you have a meeting and you don't document it, in the eyes of a regulatory agency, it never happened and you will not get "credit" for it.

In accordance with safety's best practices and OSHA guidance, every employer must provide a workplace that is safe and healthful. One way of providing such a workplace for employees is to have a comprehensive safety program that includes employee training and instructions on general and job-specific safety and health-related work practices. Many facilities routinely conduct "tailgate" or "toolbox" safety meetings or an equivalent with their employees periodically. (Personally, I like to recommend a brief, daily safety meeting [see Figure 10.1].What company doesn't have a few minutes at the start of each shift to give a safety briefing? My feeling is that if we have enough time for a coffee break, we should be able to conduct a safety briefing. Why not combine the break with the safety brief? I know that a daily meeting can be difficult for many employers, so try to compromise with a weekly safety meeting.)

The question of how often to schedule safety meetings can be the curse of facility managers. I have heard more than one manager complain, "Why do we have to talk about safety and all the bad things that can happen? It just brings up the negative, cuts into production time, and to be honest, I hate spending time on it as much as employees hate to hear it."

To some facility managers, having one safety meeting a month is too often. This makes me ask the question: How often is often enough?

First, we have to define the difference between safety training and safety meetings.

Safety training is usually formal with set schedules, goals, and objectives (such as confined-space entry, bloodborne pathogens, and ICS training) or motivational in nature to support some of these objectives. Much of this training is mandated by some regulatory authority, such as state licensing or certification, the DOT, or by your insurance carrier's requirements.

FIGURE 10.1
Workers attending a safety meeting before starting work

Safety meetings, however, are generally 10 to 15-minute opportunities (brief but informative) held to keep employees aware of potential hazards related to work-related accidents and illnesses and for managers or supervisors to discuss day-to-day hazards, use of equipment, unsafe acts, unsafe conditions, and recent incidents or near misses and to underline or review company policies or new safety rules.

Ideally, these meetings should be conducted daily (OK, how about weekly?). However, many facilities conduct monthly safety meetings and extend them to 30 minutes. Safety communication must be consistent and inclusive of all employees to be effective. Just because Julie and Bill attended a formal safety training program this month is not a good reason for the rest of your employees to miss a daily, weekly, or monthly safety meeting.

I always like to recommend that office employees be included in all of the safety meetings, because when that spill or leak call comes in, that office employee could be the most important person in your company. He or she may actually be the one to discover it, walking from one location to another to drop off paperwork.

Still, many managers would scream like a wild banshee if they had to conduct weekly safety meetings. These managers can benefit by learning communication skills that will enable them to successfully lead safety meetings.

Some managers are just uncomfortable with giving a safety talk. The fear of not being perfect might be getting in the way of important safety communication. Some managers also feel that they are not safety experts. You don't have to be.

At the same time, employees usually view a safety meeting in the same light as going to the dentist for a root canal. Who can blame employees for wanting to avoid attending safety meetings run by facility managers who probably would rather not hold them at all?

This is where senior management needs to support facility managers and supervisors by providing training on how to conduct a safety meeting. Some managers might benefit from a course in public speaking or joining a Toastmasters group.

I view manager training on how to conduct safety meetings to be as important as the operational training provided to facility employees. In order to be effective, managers must have the tools to succeed.

In my consulting, I train managers by suggesting some topics and safety meeting ideas that help to make the process relevant, interesting, and fun. Here are a few thoughts:

- Hold safety meetings in a quiet place with limited distractions (a challenge, I'm sure).
- Use newspapers, trade journal articles, case studies, and near misses to create topics.
- Start the meeting by telling employees why they are there. Define the topic and its relation to safety, accident prevention, and company policy.
- When presenting the topic, keep it short (no more than 15 minutes), positive, and fun.
- Allow time for, encourage, and reward questions—such feedback is essential.
- End the meeting by thanking employees, congratulating them on accident-free productivity, and making sure they sign the attendance sheet for your documentation.

Topics should be about health and safety issues that really exist on the job or in their particular work area. They can cover work practices, policies, procedures, machinery, tools, PPE, materials, chemicals, attitudes, and anything else that may cause or lead up to an accident or illness in the workplace.

These onsite meetings are best held at the beginning of the shift, right after lunch, or after a break; however, whatever works for your facility is what you should use for a guide. I understand that each and every facility has specific issues that it must deal with to be productive, cost-effective, competitive, and safe. At these brief meetings, employees should be encouraged to participate as much as possible, by asking questions or contributing in some manner. Meeting records should be kept stating the date, personnel present, subject(s) discussed, and corrective actions taken, if any. These records are to be maintained for the duration of each attendee's employment. Safety meeting records can also be requested for review by OSHA.

Safety meetings have proven their worth by alerting employees to workplace hazards and by preventing accidents, illnesses, and on-the-job injuries.

I have provided some resources of safety meeting topics for your use in your upcoming safety meeting. There are also some safety meeting documents that you might find useful in appendix C. Information or recommendations contained in these meeting documents were obtained from sources believed to be reliable at the time of publication. The information is only advisory and does not presume to be exhaustive or inclusive of all workplace hazards or situations. Remember, these are for brief but informative safety meetings, lasting no more than 10 minutes.

Never forget your role as a manager in preventing injuries, protecting employees, protecting customers, and protecting the bottom line.

11

Hazard Communication Standard

THE COMMUNITY RIGHT-TO-KNOW REPORTING REQUIREMENTS (see figure 11.1) build on OSHA's Hazard Communication Standard (HCS). Initially, the HCS applied only to manufacturers (designated by the Standard Industrial Classification [SIC] codes 20-39). However, in 1987, OSHA amended the regulation to incorporate all businesses, regardless of classification or size.

Under the HCS, chemical manufacturers and importers must research the chemicals they produce and import. If a substance presents any of the physical and health hazards specified in the HCS, then the manufacturer or importer must communicate the hazards and cautions to their employees and "downstream" employers who purchase/use the hazardous chemical. "Communicate the hazards" means training the workers specifically about the chemicals used at the workplace and how to use them safely and properly in processes at the workplace. This can also mean training on how to safely work near or use equipment that has hazardous chemicals contained in it that could be released into the workplace, such as an ammonia refrigeration unit that could release anhydrous ammonia in the event that the heat exchanger coils are ruptured or a valve seal fails. Workers should never be working with chemicals or equipment that they are unfamiliar with. The goal behind the HCS is to allow a safer workplace for all workers. Informed of the hazards they encounter on the job, workers and their employers can create that environment.

Protection under OSHA's HCS includes all workers exposed to hazardous chemicals in all industrial sectors. Employees have both a need and a right to know the hazards and the identities of the chemicals they are exposed to when working. Employees also need to know what protective measures are available to them to prevent adverse effects from occurring.

According to the BLS, more than 30 million workers are potentially exposed to one or more chemical hazards (www.bls.gov). Also, there are an estimated 650,000 existing hazardous chemical products, and hundreds of new ones are introduced every year. The HCS covers both physical hazards (such as flammability or the potential for explosions) and health hazards (including both acute and chronic effects).

By making information about these chemical hazards and the recommended precautions for their safe usage available to employers and employees, proper implementation of the HCS will result in a reduction of illnesses and injuries caused by chemicals. Facility managers will have the information they need to develop an appropriate protective program. Employees will be

FIGURE 11.1
Right-to-know center

better able to participate in these programs effectively when they understand the hazards involved and to take steps to protect themselves. Together, these employer and employee actions will prevent the occurrence of adverse effects caused by the use of chemicals in the workplace.

The HCS established standard requirements to make sure that the hazards of all chemicals imported, produced, or used in U.S. workplaces are evaluated and that this hazard information is conveyed to affected employers and exposed employees.

Chemical manufacturers and importers must communicate the hazard information they learn from their evaluations to downstream employers by means of labels on containers and MSDSs. In addition, all covered employers must have a hazard communication program to get this information to their employees through labels on containers, MSDSs, and training.

This hazard communication program ensures that all employers receive the information they need to inform and train their employees properly, and to design and put in place employee protection programs. It also provides necessary hazard information to employees so they can participate in and support the protective measures in place at their workplaces.

All employers, in addition to those in manufacturing and importing, are responsible for informing and training workers about the hazards in their workplaces, retaining warning labels, and making MSDSs available for hazardous chemicals.

Some employees deal with chemicals in sealed containers under normal conditions of use (such as in the retail trades, warehousing, and truck and marine cargo handling facilities). Employers of these employees must ensure that labels affixed to incoming containers of hazardous chemicals are kept in place. They must maintain and provide access to MSDSs received and obtain MSDSs if requested by an employee. They must also train workers on what to do in the

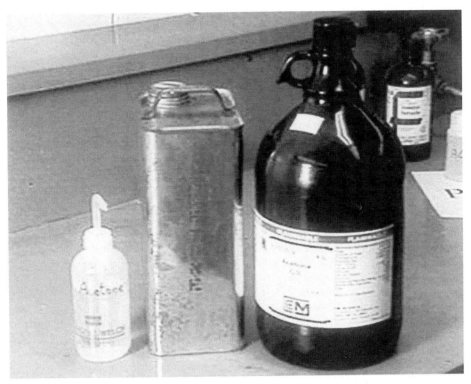

FIGURE 11.2
Containers with proper labels

event of a spill, leak, or release of the material. However, written hazard communication programs may not be required for this type of operation.

All workplaces where employees are exposed to hazardous chemicals must have a written hazard communication plan that describes how the standard will be implemented in that facility. Only certain work operations do not have to comply with the written plan requirements.

The written program has to reflect what employees are doing in a particular facility. For example, the written program must list the chemicals present at the site, indicate who is responsible for the various aspects of the program in that facility, and state where written materials will be made available to employees.

The HCS mandates the following:

- Hazard Assessment: Each employer will conduct a hazard assessment for each chemical used in the workplace.
- Inventory of Chemicals: A list of chemicals used in the workplace is to be made available to the employees.
- MSDS: An MSDS is to be made readily available for each chemical in the workplace at all times when workers are present in the facility.
- Labeling: The employer is to adopt a labeling program for each chemical used in the workplace (see figure 11.2).
- Training: The employer is to demonstrate that all employees are trained on the HCS including how to use the MSDS and the location of the MSDS.

- Written Program: Each employer is to provide a written program describing their HCSs. The written program is to be available to all employees during normal work hours.

Emergency Planning and OSHA Alliance

OSHA specifically instructs its inspectors to verify if the employer, owner, or operator has reported his or her reportable hazardous materials and coordinated its emergency action plan with the local fire department having jurisdiction.

The OSHA inspector will ask the employer if the facility has EPA reportable quantities of hazardous substances and, if they do, whether the facility notified the LEPC of the hazardous substances. The OSHA inspector will also ask the employer if the facility has experienced any chemical releases in excess of reportable quantities, and will ask for information regarding the facility's emissions inventory, if applicable. This information would establish the quantities and types of hazardous substances at a facility and provide documentation through EPA's reporting requirements. The OSHA inspectors are instructed to make referrals, as appropriate, in writing to the EPA Regional Office.

Hazard Awareness

In evaluating any work exposure the following concepts apply:

- Recognition: Recognize the hazard.
- Evaluation: Measure the hazard.
- Control: Control the hazard in the following ways:

    1. Engineering practices using Best Available Control Technology (BACT)
    2. Administrative practices (are there other less hazardous alternatives/options?)
    3. PPE

Employees must have medical clearance from a licensed physician or other licensed health care professional to wear a respirator and/or personal protective equipment. The body incurs extra physical stress during the wearing of this protective equipment, so it is important that employees be cleared by a licensed physician to undertake this additional stress. Wearing PPE may not always be completely protective. Equipment may fail, rip, tear, or otherwise be not suited for the task to be performed.

Hazards can include any of the following:

- Chemical
- Explosion and fire
- Oxygen deficiency
- Ionizing radiation
- Biological hazards
- Safety hazards
- Electrical hazards
- Heat stress
- Cold exposure
- Noise

Continuous Exposure Limits

OSHA is responsible for issuing standards and rules for safe and healthful working conditions, tools, equipment, facilities, and processes. Employers have the general duty of providing their workers a place of employment free from recognized hazards to safety and health, and must comply with all applicable OSHA standards. OSHA sets chemical exposure limits called Permissible Exposure Limits (PEL).

As additional information has gathered over time about certain chemicals, the OSHA PELs have been revised. For example, methylene chloride once had an OSHA PEL of 500 parts per million (PPM), but currently, over a period of 10 years, the PEL has been lessened to 25 PPM. Also, 1,3-Butadiene once had an OSHA PEL of 1,000 PPM, and it has been reduced to 1 PPM. That's a huge difference!

OSHA PELs are based on the concept that the worker is exposed to chemicals for no more than eight hours at a time. Thus, after work, the worker has downtime or time away from the chemicals at the facility, allowing the body time to remove or reduce the amount of chemicals. Workers who inhale chemicals at the workplace may exhale chemicals for hours after leaving work, as the body works to rid itself of them. Continuous exposure to chemicals in the workplace with no downtime does not allow for the body to cleanse itself; therefore, continuous exposure limits can cause the body to accumulate chemicals at a greater rate than they can be expelled, a potentially unhealthy or dangerous situation. OSHA PELs do not apply to continuous exposure.

Facility response personnel or others responding to a chemical spill or release should determine the OSHA PEL for the hazardous material spilled and consider the "safe" zone for the public to be at 1/100th or 1/1,000th of the OSHA PEL just to make sure it is safe. There may be quite a problem in determining exactly what chemical has been spilled, so this task for responders is not easy. The name used for the edge of the "safe" zone is the area where the chemical is below the level of concern (LOC).

Facility personnel or others responding to a chemical leak, spill, or release often consider or use another standard, the IDLH, or Immediately Dangerous to Life or Health. The IDLH level also helps emergency responders determine whether to use a respirator or what type of respirator to use. Obviously, knowing what these different standards are, what they mean, and how to interpret them is something to be done long before any accident occurs. This is another reason why chemical emergency preparedness depends on real-time, valid, facility chemical inventory information.

Other Chemical Exposure Issues

To further complicate matters, the OSHA PEL may not be an entirely correct figure. NIOSH has created standards for exposure to chemicals with RELs that are usually below OSHA PEL standards. And the American Conference of Governmental Industrial Hygienists (ACGIH) has created standards named Threshold Limit Values (TLVs) that are also generally below OSHA PEL levels.

NIOSH RELs are developed under the authority of the OSHAct of 1970. NIOSH develops and periodically revises RELs for hazardous substances or conditions in the workplace. NIOSH also recommends appropriate preventive measures to reduce or eliminate the adverse health and safety effects of these hazards. To formulate these recommendations, NIOSH evaluates all known and available medical, biological, engineering, chemical, trade, and other information relevant to the particular hazard. These recommendations are then published and transmitted to OSHA for use in promulgating (creating) legal standards. The operative word here is *recommend.* NIOSH is purely an advisory body and has no legal authority of its own. OSHA is the only agency that has the legal authority to set exposure standards, and they use the PELs to do so. The main difference between OSHA and NIOSH is that OSHA uses an eight-hour, time-weighted average, whereas NIOSH uses a 10-hour, time-weighted exposure limit. Time-weighted average means averaged over a period of time, so higher and lower exposure levels can occur.

Also, NIOSH sets "ceilings" for which exposure levels cannot be exceeded at any time. OSHA rarely sets "ceiling" exposure levels.

ACGIH TLVs refer to airborne concentrations of substances and represent conditions under which it is believed that nearly all workers may be repeatedly exposed to day after day without adverse health effects. These exposure levels are based on animal studies. With these and similar exposure standards, there is uncertainty—not a guarantee that adverse health will not result from exposure to these levels of chemicals in the air.

There are other related terms and abbreviations that may be encountered. STELs, which are Short-Term Exposure Levels (15 minutes), are based on the idea that a short-term exposure to certain levels of certain chemicals may be allowed. For the vast majority of chemicals, there simply are not enough toxicological data to warrant or establish a STEL.

TWA stands for Time-Weighted Average, which is based on the idea that exposure to levels of chemicals above the TLVs is allowed as long as the employee is subjected to periods of time during the workday when the exposure to levels of chemicals is below the Threshold Limit Values.

Occupational Standards Information

1. OSHA PELs:

   - PEL-TWA: eight-hour, time-weighted average concentration
   - PEL-STEL: 15-minute, time-weighted average concentration
   - PEL-C: Ceiling concentration, not to be exceeded

2. NIOSH RELs:

   - REL-TWA: eight-hour, time-weighted average concentration
   - REL-STEL: 15-minute, time-weighted average concentration
   - REL-C: Ceiling concentration, not to be exceeded
   - IDLH: 30-minute concentration that is immediately dangerous to life and health

3. ACGIH recommended TLVs:

   - TLV-TWA: eight-hour, time-weighted average concentration
   - TLV-STEL: 15-minute, time-weighted average concentration
   - TLV-C: Ceiling concentration, not to be exceeded

4. IDLH: The maximum level from which a worker could escape without any irreversible health effects within a 30-minute time frame

12

Hazardous Waste Operations and Emergency Response

THE HAZARDOUS WASTE OPERATIONS AND EMERGENCY RESPONSE (HAZWOPER) Standard is one of the most unique OSHA regulations, in my opinion. It is unique in two aspects. The first is that there are two training requirements in the standard (29 CFR 1910.120). The second is that the regulation actually specifies the number of training hours required for each course. No other OSHA regulation does that. Perhaps one of the most misunderstood aspects of the HAZWOPER regulation is to determine first, if it applies to your facility, and then to determine which HAZWOPER training program is required for you. This can be confusing since there are many different HAZWOPER courses, if you consider each program as having its own refresher course—a regulatory requirement! Below is a common-sense approach to the emergency response training requirements that I hope you will find useful. The hazardous waste training was discussed earlier in chapter 12.

First Responder Awareness

Does your job require your employees to be involved in emergency response to incidents where hazardous materials or chemicals are involved? For many people, the answer is yes. You might be a police officer, paramedic, emergency medical technician (EMT), firefighter, public works employee, or even a member of a Facility Emergency Response Team (FERT) at a facility where chemicals are used. If your personnel do respond to any sort of release of a hazardous material, OSHA requires that you take one of five levels of training. All of the levels start with the First Responder Awareness (FRA) course. FRA personnel are those whose jobs require them to respond to a release of a hazardous material, recognize the situation as one that requires specialized assistance, identify the material if possible, and call for help. Individuals at this level may not take any other action, except to call for help (see figure 12.1). OSHA does not give a time frame for this course.

FIGURE 12.1
A First Responder Awareness–trained employee notifying a facility manager

First Responder Operations

The First Responder Operations (FRO) course is a minimum of eight hours and builds upon the FRA course. It trains the individuals at this level to recognize and identify hazards, but also allows them to take defensive actions. By defensive actions, I mean placing spill pads, protecting storm or facility drains, shutting a valve or a switch off at a remote location, and so forth (see figure 12.2). At this level, facility personnel or others cannot become directly involved with the spill, leak, or release.

Hazardous Material Technician

The next level of training is for Hazardous Material Technicians. OSHA says that personnel trained at this level require a minimum of 24 hours of training. Many Hazardous Material Technicians attend training in excess of the 24-hour minimum, based on their response duties. Personnel trained at this level are also trained to recognize and identify hazards but also can take offensive, aggressive actions in the event of a spill, leak, or release (see figure 12.3). These actions can include:

- Plugging
- Patching
- Damming

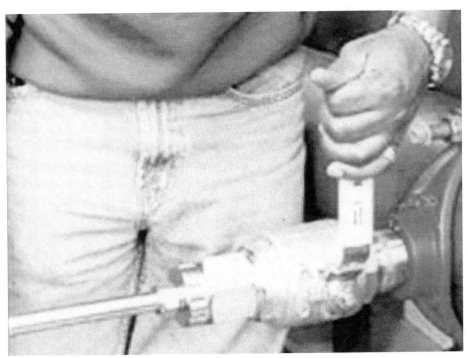

FIGURE 12.2
An operations-level trained responder shutting a valve at remote location

FIGURE 12.3
A facility emergency response team at an emergency incident

- Channeling
- Diverting
- Containing
- Confining
- Cleaning up

Hazardous Material Specialist

The Hazardous Material Specialist is a position that I don't see filled very often. I personally feel it is an important position. The specialist acts as a liaison, attempting to solve and resolve issues that may arise during a spill, leak, or release of hazardous materials. OSHA doesn't give a time requirement for this level of training; however, they state that the specialist must have the skills and knowledge of a Hazardous Material Technician, and then through education and/or experience, a person can be classified as a Hazardous Material Specialist.

Onscene Incident Commander

The Incident Commander is required by OSHA if any action is to be taken (offensive or defensive in nature) at a spill, leak, or release. Personnel trained at the Incident Commander level will receive eight hours of managing an incident, in addition to at least 24 hours of training at the

FIGURE 12.4
Incident Command Staff discussing options at an incident in New York

First Responder Operation level or the Hazardous Material Technician level. Incident Commander training is a minimum of 32 hours in length.

HAZWOPER Refresher

All persons who have taken any of the HAZWOPER training courses know that they are required to maintain their certification by taking an eight-hour annual refresher course. OSHA regulations mandate that the annual refresher course be taken prior to the expiration date of the current certificate. For many members of facility response teams, the burden of taking time away from work to meet this requirement is often very difficult; therefore, sometimes the employer actually offers the training at the facility.

A variety of topics can be offered for your annual refresher program, whether onsite or offsite. An overview of environmental regulations, toxicology, physical properties, identification systems, the HAZWOPER regulation, respiratory protection, and PPE are part of the offsite course.

13

Compliance with Occupational Health and Environmental Regulations

Several facilities that I work with implement their Environmental Health and Safety (EHS) program through a series of manuals, handbooks, and other documents, as appropriate for the operations of their particular facilities. A sample of titles of these manuals is listed below. Facility managers may be responsible for the development, distribution, and maintenance of these manuals, depending on staffing. These manuals provide specific policies and procedures and recommended practices for implementation.

- Health and Safety Management Plan
- Radiation Protection Manual
- Chemical Waste Management Manual
- Chemical Hygiene Manual
- Hazard Communication Manual
- Confined Space Entry/Rescue Manual
- Respiratory Protection Manual
- Exposure Control Plan
- Facility General Safety Manual
- Spill Prevention, Control, and Countermeasure Plan (SPCC)
- Indoor Air Quality Plan
- Hazardous Materials Emergency Response Plan
- Ergonomics Plan

These manuals provide information on EHS policies that management, staff, and visitors must follow in the workplace. The policies are intended to provide personnel with information to meet all local, state, and federal requirements for environmental compliance, occupational health, and safety.

Information on EHS training programs should also be contained in these documents or can be found by contacting the facility manager or other appropriate staff member, such as the safety manager. The facility's EHS safety programs are designed to reduce or prevent occupational injuries and illnesses through appropriate training and preventive activities.

Your Goal

I would hope that every employer believes that the health and safety of all staff and employees are of the greatest importance. Companies should conduct their operations and construct and maintain their facilities in a manner conducive to the creation of a safe and healthy work environment for all personnel, as well as the surrounding community. Through the health and safety policy, the following goals should be realized for facility employees:

- The development of an ongoing safety consciousness among all employees of the company
- A reduction in occupational injuries and illnesses and the associated loss of productivity

Safety Principles

The success of the facility's health and safety effort depends on:

- Acceptance of the concept that all serious injuries can be prevented
- Management assuming responsibility for preventing occupational injuries and illnesses
- All employees and staff participating in EHS training programs and recognizing that it is to everyone's advantage to work safely

Individual Responsibilities

All individuals who are using facility materials or equipment, working on facility property or in facility-leased space, or who are contracted to perform work on behalf of your facility have an individual responsibility to:

- Know and follow all health and safety rules, policies, and procedures for the area in which they are working
- Maintain a safe work environment
- Use good judgment
- Report to their supervisor immediately all:

  Unsafe conditions and accidents
  Work-related injuries and illnesses (every occupational accident or injury must be reported immediately to the appropriate person designated in your facility)

Employees should also know the hazards of the materials and equipment they work with and follow the specified precautions. They should properly use all safety equipment provided by the facility. In addition, they should participate as needed in exposure hazards measurement programs and safety training programs. All employees must ensure that their work activities are conducted in such a way as to not affect the safety of others.

First-Level Supervisor, Work Area Supervisor, or Manager

Managers and supervisors are responsible for being knowledgeable of and implementing applicable policies and directives and taking other action as required, ensuring that the personnel and operations they supervise comply with all applicable requirements. This includes:

- Taking positive action to determine and reduce the accidents and incidents associated with their operations
- Informing employees of the safety hazards associated with their work and work area
- Instructing employees in safe work methods
- Keeping the individual performing the specific tasks apprised of the most recent procedure and trained in its implementation
- Ensuring that employees perform their work according to requirements

Senior Facility Management

Senior staff and department heads have the primary responsibility for operations in their areas and for taking the necessary measures to make certain that all division- or department-related activities comply with established safety requirements. They shall comply with all components of the facility safety program, including all facility policies and procedures applicable to their operations, as well as other written standard operating procedures and directives.

President/Chief Executive Officer

Within the facility, the president or CEO has the ultimate responsibility for safety. That responsibility is met through having the facility manager establish requirements on all operations. There is a sample president's statement in appendix C for your review and use.

Employees

Each individual's total commitment to and enthusiastic participation in the facility's safety, health, and environmental programs are of the utmost importance, regardless of his or her length of service or position within the company. There are six major elements that should encompass the facility's EHS programs:

1. The most important element is you (the employee). You are responsible for ensuring that all of your daily work activities result in the lowest level of risk to yourself, to other personnel in your area, to the general public, and to the environment.
2. Your immediate supervisor is responsible for keeping you informed of the approved procedures and information related to the health and safety aspects of your activities.
3. In facilities with laboratories, your laboratory director, or if working with radiation, the authorized user, holds the authority for work with hazardous substances, radioactive materials, or radiation-producing devices and is therefore responsible for ensuring that all work is conducted with full regard for personnel health and safety and in accordance with the laboratory safety plan and/or the approved radiation safety plan (see figure 13.1).
4. Your department head/supervisor is responsible for establishing and maintaining a work environment that fosters the development of appropriate health and safety procedures in all activities of the department.
5. The facility manager or EHS manager administers the EHS programs of the facility. He or she provides professional assistance and expertise to the workforce community in matters relating to occupational health and safety.

FIGURE 13.1
A radiation label

6. The EHS Committee provides appropriate input to the facility manager or EHS manager and related programs. The members of this committee are drawn from the workers and staff and do not necessarily have to be recognized safety experts.

The purpose of a facility's safety programs is to provide all employees with a safe and healthy work environment; develop a safety consciousness among employees and others engaged in work for the facility; reduce accidents and occupational illnesses to a minimum; identify and control safety, public health, and environmental hazards associated with its operations; and work constructively with government agencies and others to develop laws, regulations, and standards to protect public health, safety, and the environment. Each member of the facility has the responsibility to work within the framework of established safety programs and policy. Members are also responsible for carrying out their activities in a manner that will protect those involved, the general public, and the environment.

Responding to Regulatory Agency Visits

Although visits by compliance officers from OSHA are covered elsewhere in this book, it is important to recognize that many different regulatory agencies may conduct inspections at your facility. As I mentioned, your facility is not exempt from compliance with occupational health, safety, and environmental regulations. Agencies that may conduct compliance inspections include the state Department of Health, state Department of Labor, the Department of Environmental Protection, and the Nuclear Regulatory Commission (NRC), to name just a few.

State facilities can receive fines from regulatory agencies, even though some employees may believe that as a public entity they are exempt (not true). The penalties assessed can be comparable to those assessed in the private sector.

It should be the facility's policy to comply with all applicable safety and environmental health laws and regulations and provide any appropriate documentation during compliance inspections. The facility manager or EHS manager will provide support to departments and pertinent information to the agency if an inspection occurs.

All facility employees should follow these procedures when responding to a visit from a regulatory agency. To help your facility respond to inspections, I offer the following procedures:

- Ask to see identification. All regulatory compliance officers/inspectors carry a photographic I.D. or badge.
- Wait for a representative from EHS or the facility manager before releasing any information to the inspector.
- Ask to have an opening conference and establish the nature of the visit. Request that the conference not proceed until a representative from EHS or the facility manager is present. Request specific details on the purpose of the visit (many regulatory inspections occur because of employee complaints).
- Decide the best route to the location. A tour of your facility is not advisable. Anything seen on the way to the location is also subject to inspection.
- Supply only the information requested. It is not advisable to offer more than what the inspector wants. Be courteous and provide only information that is specifically requested (i.e., just the facts—just answer the question).

The inspector has the right to interview employees, collect samples to assess exposure to chemical or physical agents, review training records and other documentation, evaluate your written safety plan to ensure compliance with various standards, take pictures, and so on. If air or other environmental samples are collected, your company should collect parallel samples to confirm or compare results. Request copies of photographs if they are to be taken; take the same pictures if you have a camera. Also, you should take very detailed notes.

In a closing meeting, after the inspection and interviews are finished, request that the inspector explain the hazard(s) involved, the corrective action(s) suggested, and a description of the violation and the applicable reference in the codes or standards.

Disciplinary Procedure

This procedure is offered to provide a guideline for the discipline of employees who repeatedly violate safety and health requirements and guides. Safety and health requirements are established and enforced to protect employees from injury and illness and to provide for a "safe and health-ful place of employment." Many facilities have a policy that applies to discipline and dismissal for violations of safety and health requirements. The basic elements of that policy are recom-mended below. In the event of any questions, your facility should seek advice from an attorney or the Human Resources manager. Management should follow the recommendations outlined in this section. Employees who violate safety and health requirements and guides should be dis-ciplined in a progressive fashion consistent with the best management practices of human re-sources as described in the following text.

First Violation

An oral warning may be given for the first violation for an environmental safety and health requirement or policy. The supervisor needs to inform the employee of the violation and the correct safe practice or procedure. The supervisor should review with the employee all applica-ble safety and health workplace requirements and policies. The employee must sign a statement indicating understanding of those requirements and procedures. The supervisor should inform the employee that any future violations may result in higher levels of discipline and may even-tually lead to dismissal.

Second Violation

The employee may be given a written warning for the second documented environmental safety and health requirement violation. This warning will specify the violation and should also refer the employee to applicable safety and health requirements and policies for review. The warning needs to also show the date the employee previously read and signed the statement of understanding of safety and health requirements and procedures. The employee, the employee's supervisor, the facility manager or EHS manager, and the employee's personnel file should re-ceive copies of the written warning.

Third Violation

The employee may be given a final warning for the third documented violation of environ-mental safety and health requirements or guides. This warning also needs to specify the viola-tion. It should also state that any further violation of safety and health requirements or guides will result in dismissal. All persons who received a copy of the written warning need to receive a copy of the final warning.

Any Subsequent Violation

The employee might be dismissed. If dismissed, the employee will receive a letter specifically identifying the violation of the environmental safety and health requirement or policy, as well as any rights of appeal through the grievance process (if any).

On occasion, an employee may commit a violation of an environmental safety and health re-quirement or policy that is so careless, reckless, willful, or so endangers life or property that it can be considered personal misconduct. When this occurs, an employee may be dismissed im-mediately, without benefit of any of the previously mentioned warnings. An employee dismissed in this fashion shall receive a letter specifically identifying the violation and detailing his or her right of appeal within the grievance procedure (if any).

General EHS Issues

Facilities might want to consider establishing administrative policies for the reduction and prevention of on-the-job accidents and illnesses and the protection of the environment. These policies can be used as a foundation for establishing safety and environmental health programs in each department or division of the facility. I believe that no job is that important and no service so pressing that facility personnel cannot take time to perform the work safely and in an environmentally conscientious manner. Companies should commit to operate their facilities and conduct their operations in compliance with all applicable regulations to protect:

- All employees
- Visitors
- Vendors or contractors
- The external community
- Natural resources and the environment

EHS Program: A Guideline to Use

The purpose of a facility's EHS program is to:

- Provide employees and staff with a safe and healthy work environment
- Develop a safety awareness among employees and others engaged in work for the facility so that accidents (personal injuries and property damage) and occupational illnesses will be reduced to a minimum
- Identify and control safety, public health, and environmental hazards associated with their operations
- Work constructively with governmental agencies and others to develop and implement laws, regulations, and standards to protect public health, safety, and the environment
- Work with the facility administration and senior managers to ensure adequate funding and staffing for EHS programs

Emergency Telephone Numbers
(For your use. Fill in the proper numbers.)
Environmental Health and Safety Manager: _____
Radiation Safety Officer: _____
Environmental Compliance and Hazardous Waste Disposal: _____
Industrial Hygiene: _____
Chemical Safety and Material Safety Data Sheets: _____

Other Safety Contacts:
Police, Fire, Ambulance, Emergency: 911or _____
Emergency Clinic/Hospital: _____
Safety Hotline to report safety problems anonymously: _____
Facility: _____

Reporting Serious Injury or Illness

In case of serious injury or illness, the immediate concern is to aid the injured or sick person. The following procedure is to be used.

Contact Public Safety immediately in one of the following ways:

- Use any cellular telephone: Dial 911.
- Use any fire alarm box in the facility.
- Use any facility phone and dial 9-911 for immediate response (see figure 13.2).

A dispatcher will answer the call and take appropriate action. A Public Safety Officer will arrive at the scene and perhaps Fire Department Emergency Medical personnel, depending on your area and the type of emergency.

Public Safety personnel have training in emergency medical care and treatment. They will take responsibility for the accident/illness scene upon their arrival. They will exercise any measure deemed necessary to sustain life or reduce further injury until the arrival of the rescue ambulance unit, if one is needed.

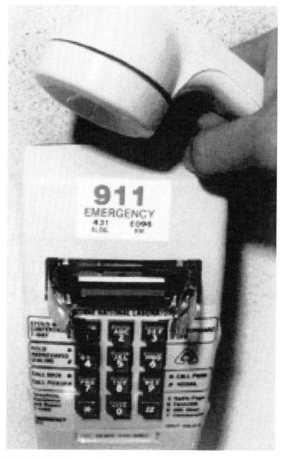

FIGURE 13.2
A 9-1-1 phone sticker on every facility phone

Reports Required by Each Facility

OSHA requires that records of all occupational injuries and illnesses be maintained and reported to employees and regulatory agencies. Required record-keeping includes:

1. A continuously maintained log of each recordable occupational injury or illness
2. A supplementary record, giving detailed data for each individual accident, injury, or illness

The facility will maintain the records noted in item 1 above. The supplementary detail record (noted in item 2) is prepared and furnished by the affected employee's supervisor or employer. These forms can be downloaded from the OSHA web site.

Prompt reporting ensures proper treatment for injuries sustained and that an investigation will be initiated as soon as possible so that:

1. Corrective measures will be taken to prevent a similar accident/incident from recurring
2. Compensation claims may be properly processed
3. Accurate facts and data are compiled

Forward the Supervisor's Accident/Incident Report form to the facility manager or Human Resources within five days. A sample form is located in the Appendix D.

Incident and accident investigations are necessary to identify accident causation and recommend corrective action(s). Therefore, supervisors must immediately investigate and report all accidents that cause injury, illness, or property loss with a written investigation report. These investigations play an important role in providing a safe working environment. Accident investigations help to identify deficiencies in the workplace and management program and to establish corrective measures to prevent accidents in the future.

It is the responsibility of management to ensure a safe and healthful work environment for their employees. Management must also comply with all company policies and government regulations. Therefore, they must investigate and report all accidents causing injury/illness or property loss immediately with a written investigation report. It is the responsibility of supervisors to complete these reports and transmit them to the facility manager and EHS. Employees are responsible to report all accidents to their supervisor.

Supervisors can help improve accident reporting in several ways:

- Train new employees to report all accidents as soon as possible, but at least before they go home for the day.
- Encourage employees to report all accidents and near misses, no matter what the case.
- Take action on all reports immediately.
- Emphasize in regular meetings with employees the importance of reporting accidents.

A successful accident investigation program contains standard investigation techniques or steps (see figure 13.3). These techniques include the following:

- Notify all pertinent personnel of accident/care for injured person(s).
- Control hazards/secure accident site.
- Investigate accident promptly.

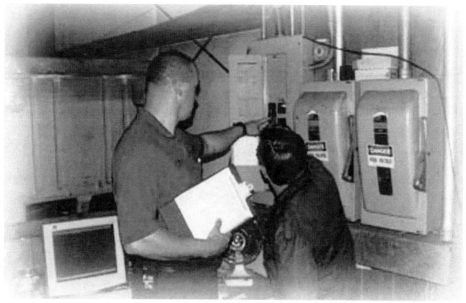

FIGURE 13.3
Investigators performing testing after an accident

- Use photographs to capture accident scene, if a camera is available.
- Use a diagram or sketch of accident site for documentation.
- Interview each employee and witnesses involved—one at a time.
- Analyze the data to identify causes and implement corrective action.
- Prepare an accident report.
- Report accident information.

When a single accident involves three or more injured persons, results in the death of a facility or contractor employee, or results in a chemical release to the environment, the supervisor must immediately notify facility manager (who has other reporting requirements). Within eight hours, the facility manager or EHS manager must notify OSHA and other necessary agencies with the pertinent information.

Occupational Accidents, Illnesses, and Reports

Some states and the Federal DOL require that your facility collect data about all occupational accidents, injuries, and illnesses to employees. The data from all such occurrences need to be compiled in several reports. These reports also initiate investigations designed to reduce both the number and severity of such incidents.

All accidents must be investigated to reduce the likelihood of repetition. Many times, a bad situation that causes a near-miss or minor accident is not corrected (or investigated) and results in a much more serious situation the second time.

The supervisor has the responsibility to investigate all accidents happening in his or her work area. Once the investigation is complete, the supervisor must fill out a Supervisor's Accident/Illness Report form (see appendix D).

In an emergency situation, the supervisor should immediately call 911. After the injured employee has been transported to an emergency facility, the supervisor should call the facility manager or Human Resources to report the work injury.

Facility Inspections

Inspections have always been the principle method of evaluating safety. The person acting as inspector (perhaps the facility manager) must examine two things to be effective: unsafe acts and unsafe conditions. Regular inspections must be conducted by facility supervisors and are routinely audited by a senior staff member or an EHS consultant; additionally, the facility inspector's supervisor should audit the inspector periodically. The supervisor must be held accountable for his or her department's safety performance.

Inspections of all facilities are the primary responsibility of the specific department head/ supervisor; the facility manager or his or her designee will perform periodic reviews to supplement these departmental inspections. Inspections should be carried out on a regular basis and documented. I have included some appropriate forms in appendix D, including annual audit forms for various issues that I found helpful, but feel free to modify or develop your own forms for inspections.

The inspector should record any observed noncompliance of safety standards and deficiency items in written inspection reports. Notification of noncompliance must be given to the department head or the appropriate supervisor for a suitable corrective action.

In the event of discovering a manipulation, action, or condition that is an imminent danger to facility personnel, the inspector should order the immediate cessation or modification of such manipulation, action, or condition. Alternatively, the inspector can request that the facility manager or EHS manger conduct an assessment. These personnel, after the assessment, are authorized to require the cessation of the hazardous condition.

The facility manager may need to notify the department head immediately of such action. If, through discussion, there is disagreement on the justification of cessation, the next level of management in both departments will need to become involved.

The facility should encourage any member of the workforce and members of the safety committee to participate in the inspection process, including citing possible violations to the inspector.

Violations and deficiencies observed by affected personnel may be reported directly to the facility manager. However, personnel should consult their supervisor first before calling the facility manager. The facility manager will then make (or cause to have) an inspection in response to such complaints. The facility manager should notify the appropriate individual(s) of the inspection results. The rights of personnel reporting complaints of matters affecting occupational safety and health or the environment shall be without retaliation on the part of any other person.

14

General Safety Topics

I COULDN'T POSSIBLY COVER EVERY ENVIRONMENTAL HEALTH and safety issue that affects the facility manager in this book. However, the following information is offered as assistance to facility managers as they deal with the day-to-day issues that face them.

General Safety Rules for Safety Equipment

Hard Hats

Facility managers should have some rules for workers to follow. Protective headgear will be worn whenever an employee's head could be endangered by falling objects, electrical shock, or impact (see figure 14.1). This requirement will be based on a job hazard analysis and can be modified at the discretion of the supervisor.

Protective headgear will be worn any time an employee enters an area declared a Hard Hat Area. Hard hats will be worn properly with the brim forward and the internal web intact (see figure 14.2 for improper usage). This is the testing configuration of the hard hats, so it needs to be worn that way, with a few exceptions. Those exceptions are:

- Welding
- Looking through a survey instrument
- The hard hat has been approved to be worn backwards—a handful of manufacturers' hats currently meet this approval.

Hard hats will not be defaced in anyway or mishandled and will be kept as clean as possible. Stickers and decals are allowed, but the hard hat cannot be totally covered since it doesn't allow for the proper inspection of the hard hat (see figure 14.3).

FIGURE 14.1
A worker wearing a hard hat properly

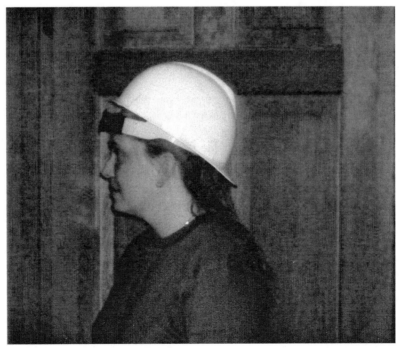

FIGURE 14.2
A worker wearing a hard hat improperly

FIGURE 14.3
Hard hats covered with decals make it difficult to inspect properly

Fluorescent Vests

Employees shall be provided with and required to wear high-visibility vests at any time they are exposed to vehicular traffic or when operating around heavy equipment. Vests must be worn in any woods operation and any time outside work is being done at night, or whenever the supervisor may deem it necessary (see figure 14.4).

Safety Foot Wear

All facility employees are advised to wear sturdy work shoes during working hours (see figure 14.5). A boot that extends over the ankle is recommended. Boots should be of high quality with sufficient ankle support to prevent twisting and sprains. Steel-toe shoes (boots) are not required by OSHA; however, they do offer greater protection for some facility personnel.

No open-toe shoes, clogs, high heels, sandals, or flip-flops are allowed on the facility property.

Gloves

Employees working in conditions that expose hands and fingers to possible cuts, burns, bruises, chemicals, or scratches are required to wear protective gloves. These conditions include:

1. Working with chemicals/recycling materials
2. Handling wood, brush, or metals
3. Handling metal, working with paint, and so on

FIGURE 14.4
Visibility garments aid equipment operators and allow others
to see the workers

FIGURE 14.5
Pair of safety shoes

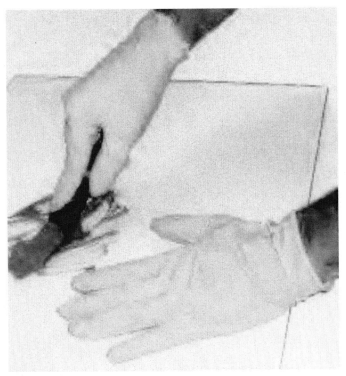

FIGURE 14.6
Worker wearing nitrile gloves to perform a task requiring gloves

This list is certainly not all-inclusive, and good judgment in the use of gloves will be expected at all times to prevent injuries to the hands and fingers.

For those workers using or handling chemicals or hazardous materials, it is expected that they will wear chemical-resistant gloves, such as nitrile gloves (see figure 14.6). Latex gloves offer no chemical protection, so do not use them for chemical handling.

Safety Glasses/Eyewear

Safety glasses, goggles, or a face shield must be worn whenever an individual is exposed to flying objects, splashes, chemicals, bloodborne pathogens, dusty conditions, or at the discretion of a supervisor. This may include, but is not limited to the following:

- Using the electric grinder or wire brush (double eye protection when grinding)
- Spray-painting
- Using the portable compressor with percussion or drilling tools
- Using the steam or spray cleaner (glasses and face shield required)
- Jump-starting a vehicle
- Using any power tool

Personnel who wear eyeglasses must wear safety glasses or goggles over them, if they are not true safety glasses with side shields (see figure 14.7). Safety lenses in your personal eyeglasses are not the same as safety glasses.

FIGURE 14.7
Safety glasses with proper side shields

Hearing Protection

Ear protection, earplugs, or earmuffs (see figure 14.8) must be worn whenever loud noise of any duration is encountered or at the discretion of a supervisor.

The use of hearing protection will include, but is not limited to the following:

- Any noise that the employee finds offensive
- Using a jackhammer or rock-drill
- Using a chainsaw or cut-off saw
- Using percussion or air tools
- Anyone working within a close proximity (30-foot radius) of equipment that requires ear protection
- Welding

Welding needs to be done in a well-ventilated area, or it requires the use of exhaust fans to remove the welding fumes (see figure 14.9). A respirator must be used when welding lasts in excess of five minutes or at the discretion of a supervisor or the facility manager.

A welding helmet and gloves must be worn when welding, and a welding screen must also be used if other employees are present in the immediate area.

All welding will be done in areas free from fire hazards and with a fire extinguisher close at hand. Some facilities may institute a fire watch program to watch for fires long after the welding (or other hot work) stops.

FIGURE 14.8
Earmuffs

Welding equipment, including a rod holder, ground clamp, cables, and connectors, has to be in good working condition and free from all defects. This equipment should be inspected prior to each use. All electrodes must be removed from the holders when left unattended.

The chipping of welding slag will require eye protection. There are no exceptions to this statement.

Hot metals from welding, cutting, or heating will be marked or cooled before being left unattended. This may be accomplished by the use of a five-gallon bucket of water in close proximity to the work site.

FIGURE 14.9
A worker welding in a facility

If there is any faulty or defective welding equipment, it should be reported to the supervisor for his or her attention.

Miscellaneous Operational Issues

Facility managers must always be observant for the "what ifs" that always seems to happen, regardless of the facility type, location, or size. Let's examine some of the major issues affecting managers.

Adverse Weather Conditions

Although we, as facility managers, cannot control Mother Nature, it is definitely an issue that can wreak havoc in a facility, depending on the time of year, location, and weather event. During adverse weather, such as thunderstorms, winter storms, heavy rain, hail events, and hurricanes, extra caution needs to be exercised when facility workers are operating company vehicles (including powered industrial trucks) or if personnel are out of vehicle performing maintenance, service, or repair work (see figure 14.10).

Electrical Lines and Overhead Obstructions

All facility workers should always assume that all wires or lines have power in them. If they are hanging down or loose, you should stay a good distance away, notify a supervisor, and/or call for help on your two-way radio or phone, if safe to do so.

FIGURE 14.10
Extra caution is needed in adverse weather

Whenever facility personnel are dealing with downed tree limbs or trees, they should always check for wires first. If wires are present, no facility personnel should touch them. They should assume they are hot and call the power company and a supervisor immediately.

Confined Spaces

Many facilities have a variety of confined spaces (tanks, manholes, vaults, etc.) in which workers may have to enter to perform work activities such as:

- Repair
- Maintenance
- Inspections/surveillance

Accessing manholes or other confined space shall be considered hazardous, and entry into these areas shall be done in accordance with the confined-space entry policy. In order for a space to be considered a confined space, it must meet all three of the following conditions (see figure 14.11). Confined space means a space that:

1. is large enough and so configured that an employee can bodily enter and perform the assigned work,
2. has limited or restricted means for entry or exit (e.g., tanks, vessels, silos, storage bins, hoppers, vaults, manholes, sewers, pits, etc.), and
3. is not designed for continuous employee occupancy.

A suggested procedure is listed below:

1. The facilities manager or his designate must determine if work in the confined space is necessary after reviewing and evaluating options.
2. If confined space work is authorized by the facilities manager or his designate, a written Confined Space Entry Permit (see appendix D) must be maintained.
3. The authorized entrant must conduct an initial atmospheric test using a device (air monitor) for that purpose prior to entering the confined space. Adequate ventilation of the confined space must also be confirmed. The authorized entrant must ensure that atmospheric oxygen content is 19.5 percent to 23.5 percent and that the LEL (lower explosive limit) is 0 percent. Otherwise entry will not be permitted unless the condition changes or proper PPE is used to safely enter the space.
4. The authorized entrant must ensure that proper PPE, if required, is available and used during the entry process.
5. While the authorized entrant is in the confined space, a standby attendant must remain outside of the confined space entry location at all times. The attendant cannot be assigned any other duties that would interfere with monitoring the confined space.

FIGURE 14.11
Workers performing a confined-space entry

6. The authorized entrant must have a means of regularly (at least every 10 minutes) communicating with the standby attendant when in the confined space area. Communication by cell phone, radio, or verbal contact is perfectly acceptable. The purpose of this is to access the condition of the individual in the confined space.
7. The standby attendant will contact 911 or Emergency Service Personnel (unless your facility has an in-house rescue team) should a rescue situation occur. The standby attendant must never enter the confined space for rescue or any other reasons. The purpose for this is that the same hazard that affected the authorized entrant may overcome the standby attendant as well.
8. If rescue services are required, the standby attendant should next contact the facilities manager. The facilities manager should notify the plant manager, the EHS manager, and other appropriate personnel as necessary.

Particulates and Dust

In the event of dusty conditions at the facility, all vehicles should be operated with the windows closed and the air-filtering systems working. This will enable work to be accomplished safely, while limiting the exposure to workers.

When there is dust in the air in employees' workstations or areas, dust masks will be made available and may be required to be worn, depending on the situation. Fit testing is not required for dust (nuisance dust) masks. If respirators are required, employees will need to be fit tested in accordance with the facility respiratory protection standard.

Lifting

Proper techniques for lifting should always be used (see figure 14.12). If facility workers have reason to deal with heavy loads, 50 pounds or more or awkward loads, they should ask a coworker for help or should use equipment or mechanical aids to eliminate manual lifting entirely.

Never twist your back while lifting a load.

FIGURE 14.12
Proper lifting techniques

Miscellaneous Equipment Safety

Hand Tools

An effective method of accident/injury prevention for facilities is the proper use of tools and the use of the right tool for the right job.

Employees should never use unsafe hand tools. They should notify the supervisor, get a replacement, and tag the tool as "out of service" or discard with permission.

1. Impact tools will be kept free from mushroom heads.
2. Tools with wooden handles shall be kept free from splinters, and handles will fit tightly in head of tool.
3. Electric power-operated tools shall be properly grounded with the ground post on the cord intact and not removed. All power cords shall be inspected before using. Any cords with visible cuts or defects will not be used.
4. Any tool not found in proper working order, or if it develops a defect while in use, shall be immediately reported to your supervisor or appropriate manager and removed from service with an out-of-service tag on it until properly repaired.
5. All power cords and outlets will be checked quarterly to verify proper grounding and tagged with four-season inspection tape. A suggestion is to use a color-coded taping system to accomplish this requirement (e.g., green = summer, orange = fall, white = winter, and red = spring).

Chain Saw and Cut-off Saw Use

The use of a chain saw or cut-off saw by any facility employee requires the following safety equipment (see figure 14.13):

1. Hard hat
2. Goggles
3. Ear protection
4. Leg chaps
5. Boot chaps
6. Gloves

A helmet with screen and earmuffs will meet the first three requirements. Operators without training will not be allowed to operate saws.

All other employees working in the area of a chain saw will stay clear of the cutter's radius. The cutter's radius while cutting brush, lumber, or trimming is about an arm's length.

Air Compressor with Percussion Attachments

The use of a portable compressor for pavement breaking, drilling, or other percussion use will require the following:

1. Safety glasses or goggles
2. Ear protection
3. A nuisance dust mask for dusty conditions

FIGURE 14.13
A worker with chain saw and protective clothing

Anyone working within a 30-foot radius of the operator must also wear the necessary protection listed above. There will be no exceptions to this requirement.

Lockout and Tagout Program

No facility employee or contractor should undertake any work on equipment unless the equipment is fully secured against the following:

- Accidental startup
- Movement
- Release of energy that could cause injury:
  - electrical
  - mechanical
  - hydraulic
  - pneumatic
  - chemical
  - thermal

FIGURE 14.14
A tag used in LOTO

All facility departments that service or repair and maintain machines and equipment need to have a Lock-Out/Tag-Out (LOTO) program. The facility has to provide the LOTO equipment and training to ensure that a power source is isolated from equipment or machinery before any work is performed. Procedures must be strictly followed to ensure the safety of everyone working on the equipment, as well as any worker in the facility in the immediate vicinity of the equipment.

Some suggestions for your facility LOTO program are listed below.

Identify the energy sources and isolate them. Prior to beginning work on any piece of equipment that could startup, move, or release stored energy, all facility employees and contractors must lock-out or de-energize all the energy sources and isolation points as identified by the facility.

Lock out/tag out procedures

1. Verification that all potential energy sources are eliminated must be made before applying the lock and tag.
2. Maintenance staff and contractors will then lock-out any valve, switch, breaker, or other control that supplies energy to the equipment. Then, they will attach a dated and signed tag that indicates the reason for the lock-out. A minimum of one lock must be installed per different trade staff working on the piece of equipment. If more personnel are asked to work on a piece of equipment, then each will apply his or her lock to the appropriate control (see figures 14.14 and 14.15).

FIGURE 14.15
A lock used in LOTO

3. Test the controls. Before carrying out any further work on the equipment, the trades staff or contractor will test the equipment to ensure that it is in fact de-energized.
4. Perform the work. Supervisors and managers must perform regular spot-checks on job sites to see if the Lock-Out/Tag-Out program is being followed.
5. Remove locks and tag. A lock and tag will be removed only by the persons who installed them. Locks will be removed only when the persons who installed them are satisfied that it is safe to do so. The person removing the last lock will do so only when he or she is satisfied that it is safe to restart the equipment.

No one, other than the persons who installed them, shall remove a lock-out lock.

Appendix A

OSHA and EPA Regional Offices Directory

OSHA Regional Office Directory

Region I
Connecticut, Massachusetts, Maine, New Hampshire, Rhode Island, Vermont
John F. Kennedy Federal Building, Room E340
Boston, Massachusetts 02203
(617) 565-9860

Region II
New Jersey, New York, Puerto Rico, Virgin Islands
201 Varick Street
Room 670
New York, New York 10014
(212) 337-2378

Region III
District of Columbia, Delaware, Maryland, Pennsylvania, Virginia, West Virginia
3535 Market Street
Gateway Building
Suite 2100
Philadelphia, Pennsylvania 19104
(215) 596-1201

Region IV
Alabama, Florida, Georgia, Kentucky, Mississippi, North Carolina,
South Carolina, Tennessee
1375 Peachtree Street, NE
Suite 587
Atlanta, Georgia 30367
Phone (404) 562-2300
Fax (404) 562-2295

Region V
Illinois, Indiana, Michigan, Minnesota, Ohio, Wisconsin
230 South Dearborn Street
Room 3244
Chicago, Illinois 60604
(312) 353-2220

Region VI
Arkansas, Louisiana, New Mexico, Oklahoma, Texas
525 Griffin Street
Room 602
Dallas, Texas 75202
(214) 767-4731

Region VII
Iowa, Kansas, Missouri, Nebraska
City Center Square
1100 Main Street
Suite 800
Kansas City, Missouri 64105
(816) 426-5861

Region VIII
Colorado, Montana, North Dakota, South Dakota, Utah, Wyoming
1999 Broadway
Suite 1690
Denver, Colorado 80202-5716
(303) 844-1600

Region IX
Arizona, California, Guam, Hawaii, Nevada
71 Stevenson Street
San Francisco, California 94105
(415) 975-4310
(800) 475-4019 Technical Assistance
(800) 475-4020 Complaints
(800) 475-4022 Publications
(415) 975-4319 Fax

Region X
Alaska, Idaho, Oregon, Washington
1111 Third Avenue
Suite 715
Seattle, Washington 98101-3212
(206) 553-5930

EPA Regional Offices

REGION 1
Connecticut, Massachusetts, Maine, New Hampshire, Rhode Island, Vermont
Address: JFK Federal Building
                One Congress Street
                Boston, MA 02203-0001
Telephone: 617/565-3420

REGION 2
New Jersey, New York, Puerto Rico, Virgin Islands
Address: 290 Broadway
                New York, NY 10007-1866
Telephone: 212/637-3000

REGION 3
Delaware, Maryland, Pennsylvania, Virginia, West Virginia, District of Columbia
Address: 841 Chestnut Street
                Philadelphia, PA 19107
Telephone: 1-800/438-2474

REGION 4
Alabama, Florida, Georgia, Kentucky, Mississippi, North Carolina, South Carolina, Tennessee
Address: 61 Forsyth Street, S.W.
                Atlanta, GA 30303-3104
Telephone: 404/562-9900

REGION 5
Illinois, Indiana, Michigan, Minnesota, Ohio, Wisconsin
Address: 77 West Jackson Boulevard
                Chicago, IL 60604-3507
Telephone: 312/353-2000

REGION 6
Arkansas, Louisiana, New Mexico, Oklahoma, Texas
Address: Fountain Place, 12th Floor, Suite 1200
                1445 Ross Avenue
                Dallas, TX 75202-2733
Telephone: 214/665-2200

REGION 7
Iowa, Kansas, Missouri, Nebraska
Address: 726 Minnesota Avenue
                Kansas City, KS 66101
Telephone: 913/551-7003

REGION 8
Colorado, Montana, North Dakota, South Dakota, Utah, Wyoming
Address: 999 18th Street, Suite 500
                  Denver, CO 80202-2466
Telephone: 303/312-6312

REGION 9
Arizona, California, Hawaii, Nevada, Guam, American Samoa
Address: 75 Hawthorne Street
                  San Francisco, CA 94105
Telephone: 415/744-1305

REGION 10
Idaho, Washington, Oregon, Alaska
Address: 1200 Sixth Avenue
                  Seattle, WA 98101
Telephone: 206/553-1200

Appendix B

Checklist for Respiratory Protection Programs

Check to ensure that your facility has a written respirator protection program that is specific to your workplace and covers the following:

- ❑ Procedures for selection of respirators
- ❑ Medical evaluations of employees required to wear respirators
- ❑ Fit-testing procedures
- ❑ Routine use procedures and emergency respirator use procedures
- ❑ Procedures and schedules for cleaning, disinfecting, storing, inspecting, repairing, discarding, and maintaining respirators
- ❑ Procedures for ensuring adequate air quality for supplied air respirators
- ❑ Training in respiratory hazards
- ❑ Training in proper use and maintenance of respirators
- ❑ Program evaluation procedures
- ❑ Procedures for ensuring that workers who voluntarily wear respirators (excluding filter face-pieces) comply with the medical evaluation, cleaning, storing, and maintenance requirements of the standard
- ❑ A designated program administrator who is qualified to administer the program
- ❑ Updates to the written program as necessary to account for changes in the workplace affecting respirator use
- ❑ Provided equipment, training, and medical evaluations at no cost to employees

Appendix C

Safety Program Sample Policies and Forms

SAFETY MEETING REPORT

Date: _____ Company: _____

Topic(s) Discussed: _____

_____

_____

Names of Employees Attending:

_____   _____

_____   _____

_____   _____

_____   _____

_____   _____

_____   _____

Conducted By: _____

Signed: _____

Comments/Recommendations:

_____

_____

_____

_____

_____

Safety Event Scheduling Chart

Weekly	Jan	Feb	Mar	Apr	May	Jun	Jul	Aug	Sept	Oct	Nov	Dec
Weekly Safety Inspection												
Weekly Boiler Checks												
Atmospheric Monitoring												
Monthly												
Compile Safety Training Report												
Fleet Driver Safety Training												
Safety Committee Inspection												
Safety Committee Meeting												
Fire Prevention Inspection												
Respirator Inspections												
Spill/Hazmat Equipment Inventory												
Fire Extinguisher Inspection												
Monthly Boiler Inspection												
Boiler Chemistry Report												
Monthly Sprinkler Inspection and Test												
Test Emergency Lighting												
Semi-Annual												
Fire Department Tour of Plant												
Emergency Lighting 90-Minute Test												
Evacuation Drill												
Boiler External Inspection												
Boiler Internal Inspection												
Annual	Jan	Feb	Mar	Apr	May	Jun	July	Aug	Sept	Oct	Nov	Dec
MSDS Audit												
Respirator Physicals												
Respirator-Fit Tests												
Noise Survey												
Hearing Tests												
Lock-Out/Tag-Out Verification and Certifications												
Boiler Safety Valve Test												
Emergency Plan Review												
Fire Hydrant Flow Test												
Forklift/Loader Recertification												
Annual Sprinkler Inspection and Tests												
Annual Training												
First Aid, CPR, BBP												
Respiratory Protection												
Confined Space Entry												
Ergonomics												
Personal Protective Equipment												
Hazard Communication												
Electrical Safety												
Lock-Out/Tag-Out												
Hearing Conservation												
Forklift Retraining												
Emergency Plans												

Weekly Safety Meeting Topics

- Asbestos Awareness
- Backs and Lifting Safely
- Bloodborne Pathogens
- Backing Up Safely
- Carbon Monoxide
- Conveyors
- Concrete Placement
- Confined Spaces
- Cell Phone Use
- Chemical Storage Safety
- Chains and Hoisting Safety Practices
- Decontamination
- Defensive Driving
- Diesel Exhaust Issues
- Electrical Power Tools
- Electrocution
- Emergency Action Plan
- Emergency Response Roles
- Fall Protection
- Fire Protection and Prevention
- Forklift Safety
- Fundamentals of Housekeeping
- Ground Fault Protection
- Hand washing
- Hard Hats
- Hand Tools
- Hazard Communication
- Hazardous Material Use/Safety
- X-ray Safety

Sample Safety Meeting Document

Safety and Saving Time

Time, in any facility, is money: Wasted Time = Wasted Money. So it goes without saying that the key to a profitable facility is getting work done "on-time" and/or within budget. But getting the work done faster does NOT mean getting it done in a manner that is not safe. To ensure that time is used to its best and that the work place remains safe, use the following, time-saving tips.

1. Keep a neat and orderly work site. People should have the responsibility of keeping their work place clean so other workers don't have to climb or walk around discarded materials, debris, and waste. Make it an ongoing process and don't leave the mess to clean up at the end of the day, because it won't get done! A clean facility is generally a safe facility.
2. Send any unused material back to the proper storage location as soon as possible. This keeps the facility clean and orderly and gives management the opportunity to use the materials in another area where they are needed.
3. Don't overcrowd materials and workers. Give the workers room to work; they will work quicker and safer.
4. Make sure that all employees understand that it is everyone's responsibility to maintain good housekeeping standards.
5. Always keep an eye out for the little thing that may cause an accident; an accident is Lost Time, Big Time.
6. Keep the tool boxes and storage cabinets neat and orderly. It doesn't take much to realize that searching around for a misplaced tool or part is lost time. And using the wrong tool/part because you could not find the right tool is, in most all cases, unsafe and against good practices and company policy.

All this boils down to one simple statement that we have all heard over and over again: "Put Things Where They Belong." By doing so, you will be using time to its best, and you will make the job easier, smoother, quicker . . . and safer.

Safety Meeting Sample

Material Safety Data Sheets

Material Safety Data Sheets, commonly called MSDSs, have come to be very important documents. Every workplace should have readily accessible MSDSs for all the hazardous materials that are used or stored there. This week's Tail-Gate Safety Topic takes a look at the content of an MSDS and provides some other important information for using an MSDS.

First of all, the time to become familiar with a material's MSDS is long before you ever start using the material. If you have responsibility for buying hazardous materials, you should obtain a copy of the MSDS, in advance of the purchase, to review the safety information before the order is placed. Many facilities and other companies require approval of hazardous materials before they are purchased. The MSDS contains information that is very helpful in the approval process.

Once a material is brought into the workplace, everyone who uses it should review the MSDS. You wouldn't want to wait until an emergency situation to learn about the material's hazardous properties! Suppose the material catches fire, gets on you, or spills from the container, causing a bigger problem. The MSDS specifies fire-fighting procedures for the material, first aid information, health hazard data, and so on. However, your chances of successfully extinguishing the blaze, cleaning up the mess, or getting it off your skin are very small if you waste valuable time running to find and review the MSDS!

There are many other very good reasons to review the MSDS before using a material. By doing so, you will learn what personal protective equipment may be required to be worn when using the material. You will learn what conditions to avoid when working with the material, such as heat and sparks. MSDSs also inform you as to what materials should not be brought into contact with the hazardous material. The MSDS provides valuable information for storage, as well as disposal of the material.

The information on an MSDS is typically grouped into these categories:

- hazard ratings, such as National Fire Protection (NFPA) ratings
- ingredients
- name, address, and contact information of the material's manufacturer or distributor
- identity: by common name, synonyms, and chemical abstract number of the material
- physical and chemical characteristics, such as the material's appearance, odor, specific gravity, and melting point
- fire and explosion data, such as the material's flash point, explosion hazards, and recommended fire extinguishing equipment
- physical hazards, such as the material's stability, incompatible material information, reactivity, and hazardous decomposition products
- health hazards, such as inhalation and ingestion hazards, carcinogen classification, and basic first aid information
- special precautions and spill or leak procedures, such as storage, clean-up, and disposal information

- special protection information, such as personal protective equipment recommendations, including respiratory protection, gloves, eye protection, clothing, and so on.

MSDSs contain a wealth of useful information for you to use when working with a hazardous material. Remember, the best time to learn the contents of the MSDS is before you ever use the material. Another thing to be aware of is that mistakes can and do happen. If you are using a material that doesn't seem to fit the description on its MSDS, do not use the material but contact your facility's safety personnel or your supervisor immediately. There could have been a mix-up in the labeling or the information on the MSDS. The material may also be out-of-spec and could be dangerous to use as you were planning.

MSDSs have proven to be very valuable tools in protecting people from hazards. They provide a wealth of information in a convenient and easy to use form. But MSDSs are only as useful as you make them. Take the time to review the MSDSs for every hazardous material you use, and apply the information provided in the documents to your everyday work assignments.

Sample Corporate Policy Statement with Respect to Safety
(President's Statement)

The Occupational Safety and Health Act of 1970 clearly details our common goal of safe and healthful working conditions for every employee. The safety and health of our employees has always been and continues to be the first consideration in the operation of this facility.

Safety and health in our facility must be a part of each and every operation. Without question, it is every employee's responsibility, at all levels.

It is the intent of this company to comply with all local, state, and federal laws. To do this, we must constantly be aware of conditions in all work areas of the facility that can produce injuries. No employee is required to work at a job that he or she knows is not safe or healthful. Your cooperation in detecting hazards and, in turn, controlling them is a condition of your employment. Please inform your supervisor, immediately, of any hazardous or dangerous situation beyond your ability or authority to control or correct.

The personal safety and health of every employee of this facility is of primary importance. The prevention of work-related injuries and illnesses is of such consequence that it will be given precedence over operating productivity whenever necessary. To the greatest degree possible, the management of this facility will provide all mechanical and physical facilities required for personal safety and health, in keeping with the highest standards and best industry practices.

We will maintain a safety and health program conforming to the best management practices of organizations of this type. To be successful, such a program must represent the proper attitudes toward injury and illness prevention, not only on the part of supervisors and employees, but also between each employee and his or her coworkers. Only through such a cooperative effort can a safety program in the best interest of all workers be established and maintained.

Our objective is a safety and health program that will reduce the number of workplace injuries and illnesses to an absolute minimum, not merely in keeping with, but surpassing, the best experience of operations similar to ours. Our goal is nothing less than zero accidents and injuries.

———————————————————

President and CEO
ABC Corporation

Sample Safe Code of Practices

A. The following is the basic Code of Safe Practices that applies at all times to all work being conducted at this facility.

1. These safety rules are not inclusive, and all federal, state and local safety regulations shall be applicable.
2. Where a conflict exists between a federal, state, and/or local applicable safety rule, the more restrictive requirement shall be in force in the facility.

B. This is a recommended format. It is general in nature and intended as a basis for the preparation of a code of safe practices by the facility manager that fits his or her operation more exactly.

1. Hard hats shall be worn at all times in construction areas.
2. Sleeved shirts shall be worn at all times. No tanks tops are allowed.
3. Long pants shall be worn at all times. No shorts, cutoffs are allowed.
4. Sturdy work shoes or leather work boots shall be worn at all times.
5. Adequate approved eye protection shall be worn when cutting, grinding, sewing or conducting any other activity that poses a potential eye hazard.
6. Full body harness with lanyards shall be used at unprotected heights of more than 6 feet.
7. Hearing protection shall be worn when employees are exposed to noise levels requiring hearing protection as defined by federal or state health and safety standards. Typically, this is 90 decibels time weighted average (TWA).
8. Illegal drugs, alcohol, fire arms, ammunition or other dangerous substances will not be allowed in the facility or on company property.
9. Good housekeeping practices shall be maintained continually.
10. Any time work is performed overhead, the supervisor conducting such work shall erect a barricade.

   - The barricade shall consist of caution or danger barricade tape and appropriate warning signs, and lightning, if required.
   - All barricades shall be removed when not in use.
   - All affected employees shall be required to honor the barricades erected by other groups/departments in the facility.

11. All persons shall follow these safe practices rules, render every possible aid to safe operations and report all unsafe conditions or practices to the supervisor immediately.
12. Foremen/supervisors/management shall ensure that employees observe and obey every applicable facility, local, state, or federal regulation and order is necessary to the safe conduct of the work, and shall take such action as necessary to obtain compliance.
13. All employees shall be given frequent accident prevention instruction. Although daily instruction is preferred, instruction shall be given at least every five work days (safety meetings).
14. Anyone known to be under the influence of drugs, alcohol, or an intoxicating substance that impairs ability to safely perform their assigned duties shall not be allowed on the job while in that condition. This should be reported to a supervisor.

15. Horseplay, scuffling, and other acts shall not be allowed in the facility under any circumstances.
16. Work shall be well-planned and supervised to prevent injuries in the handling of materials, chemicals, and in working with equipment.
17. No employee shall knowingly be permitted or required to work while his or her ability or alertness is so impaired by fatigue, illness, or other causes that the employee or others might be exposed to injury unnecessarily.
18 Employees shall not enter manholes, underground vaults, chambers, tanks, silos, or other similar spaces unless it has been determined that it is safe to enter and the employee is trained to enter the space.
19. Employees shall be instructed to ensure that all guards and other protective devices are proper and adjusted and shall report deficiencies.
20. Electric cords shall not be exposed to potential danger from vehicles, forklifts, or extensive foot traffic.
21. In locations where the use of a portable power tool is difficult, the tool shall be supported by means of a rope or similar support of adequate strength.
22. Only trained and authorized persons shall operate machinery or equipment.
23. Loose or frayed clothing, loose or hanging long hair, dangling ties, finger rings, and so on, shall not be worn around moving machinery or other areas where they man become entangled.
24 Machinery shall not be serviced, repaired, or adjusted while in operation, nor shall oiling of moving parts be attempted, except on equipment that is designed or fitted with safeguards to protect the person performing the work.
25. Where appropriate, lock-out and/or tag-out procedures shall be used.
26. Employees shall not work under areas supported by jacks or chain hoists without protective blocking that will prevent injury if jacks or hoists should fail.
27. Air hoses shall not be disconnected from compressors until the hose line has been bled.
28. Excavating, trenching, and shoring operations shall be supervised by a "competent person" (refer to OSHA regulations during all stages of field activity).
29. All excavations shall be visually inspected before backfilling to ensure that it is safe to backfill.
30. Workers shall not handle or tamper with any electric equipment in a manner not within the scope of their duties, unless they have received instructions from a qualified, licensed electrician.
31 All injuries shall be reported promptly to the foreman or supervisor so that arrangements can be made for medical or first aid treatment and documentation.
32. No burning, welding, or other source of ignition shall be applied to any enclosed tank or vessel, even if there are some openings, until it has first been determined that no possibility of explosions exist and authority for the work has been obtained from the foreman of supervisor.

Appendix C

ACKNOWLEDMENT OF RECEIPT AND
REVIEW OF CODE OF SAFE PRACTICES

TO ALL EMPLOYEES:

ATTACHED IS A COPY OF THE CODE OF SAFE PRACTICES. THESE GUIDELINES
ARE PROVIDED FOR YOUR SAFETY.

IT IS THE RESPONSIBILITY OF _____ TO
PROVIDE AND REVIEW THIS CODE WITH EACH EMPLOYEE. IT IS THE EMPLOYEE'S
RESPONSIBILITY TO READ AND COMPLY WITH THIS CODE.

THE ATTACHED COPY OF THE CODE OF SAFE PRACTICES IS FOR YOU TO KEEP.
PLEASE SIGN AND DATE BELOW AND RETURN ONLY THIS PAGE TO

_____
(Name)

I HAVE READ AND UNDERSTAND THE CODE OF SAFE PRACTICES.

_____   _____
EMPLOYEE   DATE

_____   _____
SIGNATURE   EMPLOYEE Number

Safety Audit Checklist

This safety audit checklist addresses some minimum items to be inspected. Where appropriate, the facility manager or designee may add to this checklist to include individual unique requirements or situations.

Project:_____   Location:_____

Date of Inspection:_____   Date of Last Inspection:_____

Inspection Conducted By:_____

Housekeeping/Maintenance	Y	N	Comments
Is the work area clean and orderly?	[ ]	[ ]	_____
Are floors, aisles, work areas free from obstruction and slipping and tripping hazards?	[ ]	[ ]	_____
Are floors free from protruding nails splinters, holes, and loose boards?	[ ]	[ ]	_____
Are permanent aisles and passageways appropriately marked?	[ ]	[ ]	_____
Are waste materials stored in appropriate containers and disposed of in a safe manner?	[ ]	[ ]	_____
Are guardrails or covers in place for open pits, tanks, ditches, etc.?	[ ]	[ ]	_____
_____	[ ]	[ ]	_____
_____	[ ]	[ ]	_____

Floor and Wall Openings

Are ladderways and floor openings guarded by a railing? (42" high w/midrail)	[ ]	[ ]	_____

Are open pits guarded? (standard

railing)   [ ]   [ ]   _____

Do temporary floor openings have   [ ]   [ ]   _____
standard railings or someone in
constant attendance?

Are all wall openings with a drop of [ ]   [ ]   _____
more than 4 feet guarded with a
standard railing?

Are open-sided floors, platforms,   [ ]   [ ]   _____
and runways having a drop of more
than 4 feet to the floor guarded by a
standard railing and toeboard?

Do all stairways with four or more [ ]   [ ]   _____
risers have a railing?

Are stairways strong enough?   [ ]   [ ]   _____

Are stairways too steep?   [ ]   [ ]   _____

Are stairways adequately illuminated?[ ]   [ ]   _____

Are stair treads slip-resistant? Are [ ]   [ ]   _____
the treads in good condition?

_____   [ ]   [ ]   _____

_____   [ ]   [ ]   _____

Means of Exit

Are there enough exits to allow for [ ]   [ ]   _____
prompt escape?

Are any of the exits obstructed?   [ ]   [ ]   _____

Are exits unlocked when employees [ ]   [ ]   _____
are in the building?

Are exits clearly marked?   [ ]   [ ]   _____

Are exit routes clearly marked?   [ ]   [ ]   _____

Are exits and exit routes equipped   [ ]   [ ]   _____
with emergency lighting?

_____   [ ]   [ ]   _____

_____   [ ]   [ ]   _____

Personal Protective Equipment

Is required equipment provided,   [ ]   [ ]   _____
maintained, and used properly?

Does equipment meet requirements?   [ ]   [ ]   _____
Is it reliable?

Do employees use the equipment   [ ]   [ ]   _____
whenever it's needed?

Are employees trained in the use of   [ ]   [ ]   _____
protective equipment?

Is there adequate PPE for cold season   [ ]   [ ]   _____
transition?

Employee Facilities

Is drinking water available?   [ ]   [ ]   _____

Are drinking facilities clean and sanitary?   [ ]   [ ]   _____

Are washing facilities clean and   [ ]   [ ]   _____
sanitary?

Are toilets kept clean and in good   [ ]   [ ]   _____
repair?

Are separate dining facilities provided   [ ]   [ ]   _____
in plants where toxic chemicals are
used? Do employees use them?

Are food preparation areas clean and   [ ]   [ ]   _____
sanitary?

_____   [ ]   [ ]   _____

_____   [ ]   [ ]   _____

Medical and First Aid

Are emergency phone numbers   [ ]   [ ]   _____
clearly posted?

Are there employees on each shift   [ ]   [ ]   _____
who are trained in first aid?

Are approved first-aid supplies   [ ]   [ ]   _____
readily available?

Are eye-wash stations well marked   [ ]   [ ]   _____
and full?

Are first-aid kits clean and well-   [ ]   [ ]   _____
stocked?

Are any employees trained in CPR?   [ ]   [ ]   _____

Is there adequate insect protection?   [ ]   [ ]   _____

Are 24-hour air operations available for   [ ]   [ ]   _____
fixed-wing aircraft?

_____   [ ]   [ ]   _____

_____   [ ]   [ ]   _____

Fire Protection

Are there enough fire extinguishers   [ ]   [ ]   _____
to do the job?

Are extinguishers well-marked?   [ ]   [ ]   _____

Are they properly mounted and   [ ]   [ ]   _____
accessible?

Are all extinguishers fully charged   [ ]   [ ]   _____
and operable?

Are special-purpose extinguishers clearly marked?	[ ]	[ ]	_____
Are there smoke detectors installed?	[ ]	[ ]	_____
Have smoke detectors been tested? Date:_____	[ ]	[ ]	_____
Is there a fire alarm system? Has it been tested? Date:_____	[ ]	[ ]	_____
_____	[ ]	[ ]	_____

Materials Handling and Storage

Is materials handling equipment in good condition?	[ ]	[ ]	_____
Is all hazardous and toxic material handled, stored, and transported in accordance with regulatory requirements?	[ ]	[ ]	_____
Is adequate clearance allowed in aisles where your material must be moved?	[ ]	[ ]	_____
Are storage areas properly illuminated?	[ ]	[ ]	_____
Are cylinders transported and stored in upright position and properly secured?	[ ]	[ ]	_____
Are tiered materials stacked, interlocked, locked, and limited in height to maintain stability?	[ ]	[ ]	_____
Are storage areas kept free of tripping, fire, explosion, and pest hazards?	[ ]	[ ]	_____
Is proper drainage provided?	[ ]	[ ]	_____

Are signs posted warning of   [ ]   [ ]   _____
clearance limits?

_____   [ ]   [ ]   _____

_____   [ ]   [ ]   _____

Hand and Portable Power Tools

Are correct tools provided?   [ ]   [ ]   _____

Are hand tools and power equipment
in good condition?   [ ]   [ ]   _____

Are guards in place and adjusted   [ ]   [ ]   _____
properly?

Are electric tools protected by GFCI? [ ]   [ ]   _____

Have all electric tools been checked [ ]   [ ]   _____
for ensured grounding?

_____   [ ]   [ ]   _____

_____   [ ]   [ ]   _____

Machinery and Equipment

Is all equipment in safe operating   [ ]   [ ]   _____
condition?

Are all machines guarded to protect [ ]   [ ]   _____
operators from hazards?

Are equipment operators properly   [ ]   [ ]   _____
attired (no loose clothing, jewelry;
long hair tied back or tucked in)?

Are point-of-operation guards in place [ ] [ ]   _____
on all operating equipment?

Are all belts and pulleys less than 7 [ ]   [ ]   _____

feet from the floor guarded?

Are spinning parts guarded?   [ ]   [ ]   _____

Are proper tools provided for   [ ]   [ ]   _____
cleanup and adjustment of machinery?

_____   [ ]   [ ]   _____

Electrical

Are all switches and breakers   [ ]   [ ]   _____
properly identified?

Are motors clean and free of oil,   [ ]   [ ]   _____
grease, and dust?

Are all machines properly grounded?   [ ]   [ ]   _____

Are portable hand tools grounded or   [ ]   [ ]   _____
double-insulated?

Are junction boxes closed?   [ ]   [ ]   _____
Are extension cords out of the aisles   [ ]   [ ]   _____
where they may be damaged by
heavy traffic?

Are extension cords being used as   [ ]   [ ]   _____
permanent wiring?

_____   [ ]   [ ]   _____

_____   [ ]   [ ]   _____

Hazard Communication

Is there an MSDS for every   [ ]   [ ]   _____
chemical in the workplace? (spot-
check on each inspection, complete
chemical inventory each year).

Are labels prominently displayed   [ ]   [ ]   _____
on containers?

Are the labels legible?   [ ]   [ ]   _____

Does each label contain at least   [ ]   [ ]   _____
the chemical name, any necessary
hazard warnings, and first-aid procedure?

Are MSDS sheets readily available   [ ]   [ ]   _____
to all employees in the workplace
during all shifts?

_____   [ ]   [ ]   _____

_____   [ ]   [ ]   _____

Additional comments:

_____

_____

_____

CONTRACTOR'S ASBESTOS SAFETY INSPECTION CHECKLIST

The facility manager/designee should complete a safety inspection of the contractor's job on a weekly frequency and file the inspection results with the contractor's job records.

		OK	US	NR
Date:				
Project Title:	License			
Contractor:	Respirator-Fit Tests			
Project Manager:	Training Records			
Audit Conducted By:	Physicals			
Number of Employees Working on Job:	Estimated Size of Job: _____ lineal ft			

OK = Satisfactory Condition; US = Unsatisfactory Condition; NR = Not Required

I. Personal Protection	OK	US	NR		OK	US	NR
Safety Glasses				Respirators			
Shoes				Hearing Protection			
Clothing				Hard Hat			
Gloves							

II. Equipment	OK	US	NR		OK	US	NR
Ladders				Scaffolding			
Electrical Cords				Lift Trucks			
Ground Fault Interrupts				HEPA Vacuum			
Safety Harnesses				Water Sprayer			

III. Housekeeping	OK	US	NR	IV. Work Practices	OK	US	NR
Landfill				Elevated Work			
Work Area (Job Site)				Work around hot pipes			
Office				Safety flagging			
Shop							

Comments: _____

V. Containment Projects	OK	US	NR		OK	US	NR
Negative Air Machines				Water Filter			
Pressure				Respirators			
Shower				Ambient Air Testing			
Construction Requirements				Warning Signs			

Comments: _____

VI. Glovebag Projects	OK	US	NR		OK	US	NR
Area Secured				Respirators			
Warning Signs				Clothing			
Barrier Tape				Portable Shower			
Ambient Air Testing							

Comments: _____

_____	_____
Contractor Coordinator	Date

Appendix D
Sample Audit Forms

Annual Safety Audit

Facility _____ Area _____

Auditor _____ Date _____

Area	Satisfactory	Action Required	Corrective Action (date)
Safety Officer			
Person assigned			
Written job description			
Written Program			
Safety policy statement			
Written programs			
Responsibilities defined			
Safety plan of action			
Safety rules			
Operating procedures posted			
Administrative procedures			
Written fire prevention plan			
Written emergency plan			
Management Responsibility			
Sufficient staff and resources			
Management commitment			
Communication w/ employees			
Program Enforcement			
Written enforcement policy			
Records of disciplinary action			
Managers held accountable			
Hazard Identification			
Department inspections			
Hazard analysis for each task			
Purpose inspections			
Safety reviews for changes			
Hygiene inspections			
Hazard control procedures			

Hazard Control			
All hazards classified			
No employee in hazard areas			
Correction documentation			
Corrective actions taken			
Personal Protective Equipment Program			
Hazard analysis completed			
PPE assessment completed			
Replacement as required			
Adequate stocks available			
Training completed			
Communication			
Periodic safety communication			
Means for communication			
Employee participation			
Training			
Safety orientation program			
Preassignment task training			
Annual retraining			
Training records maintained			
Supervisors training			
Specialized training			
Accident Investigation and Corrective Action			
Supervisors trained			
Accident investigation forms			
All accidents investigated			
Corrective actions identified			
Corrective actions taken			
Written records			
Trends evaluated			
First-aid responders trained			

Notes:

CONFINED-SPACE ENTRY AUDIT			
Entry Location:			
Audit Date: _____ Auditor: _____			
TRAINING DATES (enter the dates that the Entry Team was trained)	Attendant(s): Entrant(s): Supervisor:		Comments
KNOWLEDGE When questioned, does the CSE Team understand their specific duties?	YES	NO	Comments
ATMOSPHERE Has the atmosphere been checked? Rechecked? Is the person performing the atmospheric test qualified? Has the equipment been calibrated?	YES YES YES YES	NO NO NO NO	Comments
LOTO/TRY Has all applicable LOTO/Try or isolation procedures been completed? Has the LOTO/Try checklist been filled out correctly?	YES YES	NO NO	Comments
ADDITIONAL PERMITS Are any additional permits required? If so, are they filled out correctly?	YES YES	NO NO	Comments
SIGNAGE Has the CSE been designated by the use of a sign?	YES	NO	Comments

COMMUNICATION			Comments
Is the CSE communication system in place?	YES	NO	
RESCUE			Comments
Has the CSE rescue group been contacted?	YES	NO	
Is a retrieval system needed?	YES	NO	
If so, is it in place?	YES	NO	
Do team members know their rescue duties?	YES	NO	

Electrical Safety Audit

Facility _____ Area _____

Auditor _____ Date _____

Area	Satisfactory	Action Required	Corrective Action (date)
Employee Knowledge			
Date of electrical safety training			
Hazards of Electricity			
Reporting electrical hazards			
Safe electrical work practices			
Program Administrative			
Last elect. safety inspection			
Written program			
Qualified electricians			
Training certificates			
Safeguards			
Engineering safeguards			
Administrative safeguards			
Training safeguards			
Electrical Safety Equipment			
Lock-out/Tag-out material			
Volt/Ohm meters			
Electrical-rated gloves			
Electrical-rated rubber matting			
Insulated tools			
Barriers and signs			

Nonconductive ladders			

Area Inspection

Electrical services labeled			
No missing knockout plugs			
No exposed wires or circuits			
Grounded plugs			
Wiring is in permanent conduit			
Extension cords from above have strain-relief fasteners			
No cords through doors, windows, or walls			
Free clearance and approach to electrical panels			

Operational Questions

	Do you specify compliance with OSHA for all contract electrical work?
	Are all employees required to report as soon as practicable any obvious hazard to life or property observed in connection with electrical equipment or lines?
	Are employees instructed to make preliminary inspections and/or appropriate tests to determine what conditions exist before starting work on electrical equipment or lines?
	When electrical equipment or lines are to be serviced, maintained, or adjusted, are necessary switches opened, locked-out, and tagged whenever possible?
	Are portable electrical tools and equipment grounded or of the double insulated type?
	Are electrical appliances such as vacuum cleaners, polishers, and vending machines grounded?
	Do extension cords being used have a grounding conductor?
	Are multiple-plug adaptors prohibited?

	Are ground-fault circuit interrupters installed on each temporary 15 or 20 ampere, 120 volt AC circuit at locations where construction, demolition, modifications, alterations, or excavations are being performed?
	Are all temporary circuits protected by suitable disconnecting switches or plug connectors at the junction with permanent wiring?
	Do you have electrical installations in hazardous dust or vapor areas? If so, do they meet the National Electrical Code (NEC) for hazardous locations?
	Is exposed wiring and cords with frayed or deteriorated insulation repaired or replaced promptly?
	Are flexible cords and cables free from splices or taps?
	Are clamps or other securing means provided on flexible cords or cables at plugs, receptacles, tools, equipment, etc., and is the cord jacket securely held in place? Are all cord, cable, and raceway connections intact and secure?
	In wet or damp locations, are electrical tools and equipment appropriate for the use or location or otherwise protected?
	Is the location of electrical power lines and cables (overhead, underground, under floor, other side of walls) determined before digging, drilling, or similar work is begun?
	Are metal measuring tapes, ropes, handlines or similar devices with metallic thread woven into the fabric prohibited where they could come in contact with energized parts of equipment or circuit conductors?
	Is the use of metal ladders prohibited in areas where the ladder or the person using the ladder could come in contact with energized parts of equipment, fixtures, or circuit conductors?
	Are all disconnecting switches and circuit breakers labeled to indicate their use or equipment served?
	Are disconnecting means always opened before fuses are replaced?
	Do all interior wiring systems include provisions for grounding metal parts of electrical raceways, equipment, and enclosures?
	Are all electrical raceways and enclosures securely fastened in place?
	Are all energized parts of electrical circuits and equipment guarded against accidental contact by approved cabinets or enclosures?
	Is sufficient access and working space provided and maintained about all electrical equipment to permit ready and safe operations and maintenance?

☐	Are all unused openings (including conduit knockouts) in electrical enclosures and fittings closed with appropriate covers, plugs, or plates?
☐	Are electrical enclosures, such as switches, receptacles, and junction boxes provided with tight-fitting covers or plates?
☐	Are disconnecting switches for electrical motors in excess of two-horsepower capable of opening the circuit when the motor is in a stalled condition without exploding? (Switches must be horsepower rated equal to or in excess of the motor hp rating.) Is low-voltage protection provided in the control device of motors driving machines or equipment that could cause probable injury from inadvertent starting?
☐	Is each motor disconnecting switch or circuit breaker located within sight of the motor control device?
☐	Is each motor located within sight of its controller or the controller disconnecting means capable of being locked in the open position or is a separate disconnecting means installed in the circuit within sight of the motor?
☐	Is the controller for each motor in excess of two horsepower, rated in horsepower equal to or in excess of the rating of the motor it serves?
☐	Are employees who regularly work on or around energized electrical equipment or lines instructed in the cardiopulmonary resuscitation (CPR) methods?
☐	Are employees prohibited from working alone on energized lines or equipment over 600 volts?

Notes

Fire Prevention Audit

Facility _____ Area _____

Auditor _____ Date _____

Area	Satisfactory	Action Required	Corrective Action (date)
Employee Knowledge			
Date of prevention training			
Date of last drill			
Housekeeping rules			
Use of fire extinguishers			
Evacuation procedure			
High hazard areas			
High hazard tasks			
Program Administration			
Written fire prevention plan			
Lists high hazard areas			
Lists sources of combustion			
Lists means to control sources			
Welder training			
Monthly sprinkler inspection			
Annual sprinkler system test			
Fire department has toured			
Emergency phone # posted			
Written hot work program			
Safeguards			
Engineering safeguards			
Administrative safeguards			
Training safeguards			
Area Inspection			
Proper material storage			
No combustible scrap			
Approved containers			
No Smoking signs posted			
Fire extinguishers checked			
Fire extinguishers available			
Notes			

Flammable Liquid Storage Audit

Facility _____ Area _____

Auditor _____ Date _____

Area	Satisfactory	Action Required	Corrective Action (date)
Employee Knowledge			
Date last fire prevention training			
Proper use and storage			
Spontaneous combustion hazards			
Hot work training completed			
Use of grounding straps			
Program Administration			
Fire prevention plan reviewed			
No Smoking rules enforced			
Safeguards			
Engineering safeguards			
Administrative safeguards			
Training safeguards			
Area Inspection			
Combustible scrap, debris, and waste materials (oily rags, etc.) stored in covered metal receptacles and removed from the worksite promptly			
Approved containers and tanks used for the storage and handling of flammable liquids			
No leaks on connections on drums and combustible liquid piping			
Flammable storage lockers vented to outside			
Flammable liquids containers closed when not in use (for example, parts cleaning tanks, pans, etc.)			

No combustible flammables in designated welding areas			
Bulk drums grounded and bonded to containers during dispensing			
Flammable liquid storage rooms have explosion-proof lights			
Storage rooms have adequate ventilation			
No Smoking signs posted on liquefied petroleum gas tanks			
Liquefied petroleum storage tanks guarded to prevent damage from vehicles			
Solvent wastes and flammable liquids kept in fire-resistant, covered containers			
Fuel gas cylinders and oxygen cylinders separated by distance and fire-resistant barriers			
Fire extinguishers within 75 feet of outside flammable liquids storage areas and within 10 feet of inside storage areas			
No Smoking signs posted in areas where flammable or combustible materials are used or stored			
Safety cans for dispensing flammable or combustible liquids at a point of use			
Spills cleaned up promptly			
Storage tanks vented to prevent excessive vacuum or pressure			
Storage tanks equipped with emergency venting			

Lock-out/Tag-out Audit

Facility _____ Area _____

Auditor _____ Date _____

Area	Satisfactory	Action Required	Action completed
Employee Knowledge			
Date of training			
Purpose of LOTO			
Devices used			
Procedure location			
Energy control methods			
Programs Administration			
Training certificates			
Annual review of program			
Equipment procedures			
Annual proficiency review			
List of locks issued			
Safeguards			
Engineering safeguards			
Administrative safeguards			
Training safeguards			
Area Inspection			
Standardized locks and tags			
Locks issued to individuals			
Notification procedures			
LOTO procedure used			
Sufficient devices available			

Operational Questions	
	Is all machinery or equipment capable of movement required to be de-energized or disengaged and locked-out during cleaning, servicing, adjusting, or setting up operations, whenever required?
Where the power disconnecting means for equipment does not also disconnect the electrical control circuit:	
	Are the appropriate electrical enclosures identified?
	Is means provided to assure the control circuit can also be disconnected and locked-out?

	Is the locking-out of control circuits in lieu of locking-out main power disconnects prohibited?
	Are all equipment control valve handles provided with a means for locking-out?
	Does the lock-out procedure require that stored energy (mechanical, hydraulic, air, etc.) be released or blocked before equipment is locked-out for repairs?
	Are appropriate employees provided with individually keyed personal safety locks?
	Are employees required to keep personal control of their key(s) while they have safety locks in use?
	Is it required that only the employee exposed to the hazard, place or remove the safety lock?
	Is it required that employees check the safety of the lock-out by attempting a startup after making sure no one is exposed?
	Are employees instructed to always push the control circuit stop button immediately after checking the safety of the lock-out?
	Is there a means provided to identify any or all employees who are working on locked-out equipment by their locks or accompanying tags?
	Are a sufficient number of accident preventive signs or tags and safety padlocks provided for any reasonably foreseeable repair emergency?
	When machine operations, configuration, or size requires the operator to leave his or her control station to install tools or perform other operations, and that part of the machine could move if accidentally activated, is such element required to be separately locked or blocked out?
	In the event that equipment or lines cannot be shut down, locked-out, and tagged, is a safe job procedure established and rigidly followed?

Notes

Personal Protective Equipment Audit

Facility _____ Area _____

Auditor _____ Date _____

Area	Satisfactory	Action Required	Corrective Action (date)
Employee Knowledge			
Date last PPE training			
When to use PPE			
Limitations			
Selection and Inspection			
Cleaning and storage			
Donning and removal			
Program Administration			
Hazard assessment completed			
Hazard control survey completed			
PPE hazard certification completed			
High hazard areas identified			
PPE disposal procedures			
Safeguards			
Engineering safeguards			
Administrative safeguards			
Training safeguards			
Area Inspection			
Signs and warnings posted			
Adequate PPE stock available			
Electricians wear electrically rates safety shoes/hard hats			
PPE clean and properly stored			
PPE used properly			

	Operational Questions
	Is there a hazard assessment procedure used to determine if hazards that require the use of personal protective equipment (for example, head, eye, face, hand, or foot protection) are present or are likely to be present?
	If hazards or the likelihood of hazards are found, is PPE selected and are affected employees properly fitted for the personal protective equipment suitable for protection from these hazards?
	Have employee been trained on PPE procedures, that is, what PPE is necessary for a job task, when they need it, and how to properly adjust it?
	Are protective goggles or face shields provided and worn where there is any danger of flying particles or corrosive materials?
	Are approved safety glasses required to be worn at all times in areas where there is a risk of eye injuries such as punctures, abrasions, contusions, or burns?
	Are employees who need corrective lenses (glasses or contacts) in working environments having harmful exposures, required to wear only approved safety glasses, protective goggles, or other medically approved precautionary procedures?
	Are protective gloves, aprons, shields, or other means provided and required where employees could be cut or where there is reasonably anticipated exposure to corrosive liquids, chemicals, blood, or other potentially infectious materials?
	Are hard hats provided and worn where danger of falling objects exists?
	Are hard hats inspected periodically for damage to the shell and suspension system?
	Is appropriate foot protection required where there is the risk of foot injuries from hot, corrosive, or poisonous substances, falling objects, crushing, or penetrating actions?
	Are approved respirators provided for regular or emergency use where needed?
	Is all protective equipment maintained in a sanitary condition and ready for use?
	Are there eye-wash facilities and a quick drench shower within the work area where employees are exposed to injurious corrosive materials? Where special equipment is needed for electrical workers; is it available?
	Where food or beverages are consumed on the premises, are they consumed in areas where there is no exposure to toxic material, blood, or other potentially infectious materials?
	Is protection against the effects of occupational noise exposure provided when sound levels exceed those of the OSHA noise standard?
	Are adequate work procedures, protective clothing, and equipment provided and used when cleaning up spilled toxic or otherwise hazardous materials or liquids?
	Are there appropriate procedures in place for disposing of or decontaminating personal protective equipment contaminated with, or reasonably anticipated to be contaminated with, blood or other potentially infectious materials?

Respiratory Protection Audit

Facility _____ Area _____

Auditor _____ Date _____

Area	Satisfactory	Action Required	Action Completed
Employee Knowledge			
Date training			
Respiratory hazards			
Locations and tasks requiring respirators			
Selection of respirators			
Donning procedures			
Fit checks			
Respirator limitations			
Removal procedures			
Clean, inspect, and store			
Program Administration			
Written program			
Change-out schedule			
Respiratory physicals			
Fit-test certificates			
Hazard assessment			
Manufacturers instructions			
Designated administrator			
Safeguards			
Engineering safeguards			
Administrative safeguards			
Training safeguards			
Area Inspection			
Signs posted			
Proper storage			
Cleaning material available			
SCBAs checked per manufacturers instruction			
Proper canisters and filters available			
Respirators in good repair			
Fit-test equipment			

Safety Tour Checklist

Job Site Name: _____   Date: _____

All items must be checked. If a deficiency is found, the date corrections will be made and the person making the corrections must be noted for that item.

_____

	Yes	No	Correction Date
1. A. MSDS manual readily available?	___	___	_____
B. Job-specific chemical list complete and filed in book?	___	___	_____
C. Job-specific MSDSs filed in book as shown on list?	___	___	_____
D. HazCom training taking place and documented?	___	___	_____
2. A. Assigned Safety Coordinator on job?	___	___	_____
B. Name of Safety Coordinator_____			
3. A. Monthly site inspection report forms on job?	___	___	_____
B. Inspections being done monthly and documented?	___	___	_____
C. Copies sent to company office?	___	___	_____
D. Deficient items being followed up?	___	___	_____
E. Corrections noted and dated on field copy of form?	___	___	_____
4. A. The following personal protective equipment (PPE) available on job:			
Safety glasses?	___	___	_____
Chemical PPE (face shield, rubber gloves, rubber apron)?	___	___	_____
Safety harness if applicable?	___	___	_____
B. PPE being worn?	___	___	_____
5. Tools and cords (GFI)being used in good repair?	___	___	_____
6. Safety guards on equipment?	___	___	_____
7. Work areas are well-lit?	___	___	_____
8. Floors and work areas are clean and neat?	___	___	_____
9. Floors free of slipping hazards (water, oil, etc.)?	___	___	_____
10. Tripping hazards in the work areas have been eliminated?	___	___	_____
11. Conditions of concrete floors and stairs or wood stairs are free from defects which would create a workplace hazard?	___	___	_____
12. Equipment and parts stored properly?	___	___	_____
13. Proper work uniforms/shoes being worn?	___	___	_____
14. Stairways and door openings viewed are free from obstruction?	___	___	_____
15. Fire doors are not propped open and are closed and latched?	___	___	_____
16. Electrical rooms are clean and clear of improperly stored materials?	___	___	_____
17. Proper clearance in front of power panels and switchgear (3 ft)?	___	___	_____
18. Safety lock-out of equipment during repairs is being practiced?	___	___	_____
19. Ladders inspected were free from defects and are safe to use?	___	___	_____
20. Proper eye protection is provided near grinders, welding, and burning equipment and at chemical stations?	___	___	_____
21. Proper functioning eye-wash stations and adequate stations present?	___	___	_____
22. Equipment is free from oily surfaces and/or leaks?	___	___	_____
23. Equipment, pipes, or valves are all free from steam and water leaks?	___	___	_____

Comments:

Remember to follow up on deficiencies.

Inspector:_____Date:_____

Copies to:_____Date:_____

Deficiencies corrected:_____Date:_____

Hazardous Waste Storage Area Weekly Inspection Checklist

Inspector Name: _____   Date: _____ Time: _____

Location of Inspection: _____   Total Number of Containers: _____

		YES	NO
1.	Is the area free from debris and other materials?	☐	☐
2.	Is the ground clean and dry?	☐	☐
3.	Are container tops free from spillage?	☐	☐
4.	Is the area free from spills or leaks?	☐	☐
5.	Are all of the containers in good condition? (free from dents and corrosion, not bulging, or otherwise deteriorating?)	☐	☐
6.	Are all containers properly closed?	☐	☐
7.	Are containers labeled with hazardous waste labels?	☐	☐
8.	Is the following information on the labels filled out?		
	Generator name and address	☐	☐
	Accumulation start date	☐	☐
	Contents	☐	☐
	Physical state	☐	☐
	Hazardous properties	☐	☐
9.	Is the information on the labels legible?	☐	☐
10.	Have wastes been disposed of within the allowable accumulation time?	☐	☐
11.	Are the containers compatible with their contents?	☐	☐
12.	Are incompatible wastes stored separately?	☐	☐
13.	Is there adequate aisle space?	☐	☐

Describe any observations for items checked NO. _____

_____

_____

_____

_____

Corrective actions required.   _____

_____

_____

Chemical Use in Facility Areas
Self-Audit Checklist

Building _____   Room _____

Supervisor _____

Date _____

Audit Performed by _____

	Y	N	NA	COMMENTS
A. General Work Environment				
1. Work areas illuminated				
2. Storage of combustible materials minimized				
3. Trash removed promptly				
4. Aisles and passageways kept clear				
5. Wet surfaces covered with nonslip material				
6. Heavy items stored on lower shelves				
7. Means available to reach items stored above shoulder level				
8. Storage at least 18 inches below sprinkler head				
9. Storage at least 24 inches below ceiling				
10. Exits				
a. Illuminated signs working				
b. Paths free from obstruction				
c. Alternate exits available				
d. Fire doors not blocked or wedged open				
e. Doors not locked				
11. Pits and floor openings covered or guarded				

B. Emergency Planning				
Facilities				
1. Fire extinguishers mounted near doorway				
2. Fire extinguishers unobstructed				
3. Fire extinguisher fully charged				
4. Fire extinguisher tamper indicator in place				
5. Eye-wash and safety showers available in close proximity and unobstructed				
6. Fire alarm pull stations unobstructed				
7. Emergency lights functional				
Inspections				
8. Fire extinguisher inspected				
9. Eye-wash and safety shower inspected				
Procedures				
10. Spill control plan completed				
11. Spill control materials available and adequate to cover anticipated spills				
C. Required Information/Postings				
Information				
1. Written emergency action plan				
2. Material safety data sheets readily accessible				
3. Written hazard communication program available				
4. Written respiratory protection program available				
5. Documentation of personal protective equipment hazard assessment and training				
Postings				
6. Emergency information posters accurate and current				
7. OSHA poster				
8. Telephones posted with 911 sticker				

9. Building evacuation routes posted				
10. Fire code permits posted (when required)				

D. Personal Protective Equipment

1. Eye and face protection available where needed				
a. Goggles and face shields for corrosives				
b. Industrial safety glasses for flying particles				
2. Areas requiring the use of eye protection posted				
3. Open-toe shoes prohibited in areas where corrosives are used				
4. Respirator users: a. Appropriate respirator/appropriate cartridge used				
b. User(s) enrolled in respiratory protection program				

E. Chemical Storage

Facilities

1. Shelving adequate for loads imposed				
2. Refrigeration units for chemical storage labeled "No Food"				
3. Refrigeration units for food labeled "Food Only"				
4. Chemical storage cabinets properly labeled				

Containers

5. Containers clearly labeled with chemical name(s)				
6. Containers kept closed except during transfers				
7. Containers compatible with the chemical				

Procedures

8. Chemicals segregated to avoid incompatibilities				

9. Large/heavy containers stored on lower shelves				
10. Corrosives not stored above eye level				
11. Storage quantities minimized				
12. Secondary containers used during transport of more than 1 pint of hazardous chemicals				
13. Materials with shelf lives dated and disposed of per supplier's recommendations				
14. Fire code permits obtained				
F. Flammable Liquids				
1. Used in well-ventilated area				
2. Stored in flammable liquid storage cabinet for more than 10 gallons per room				
3. Flammables separated from strong oxidizers				
4. Class ABC or BC fire extinguisher provided				
5. Flammable liquids not stored near ignition sources				

G. Compressed Gases				
1. Used in well-ventilated area				
2. Storage quantities minimized				
3. Secured from tipping in use				
4. Regulators compatible with gas cylinder				
5. Cylinder carts used for transport				
6. Protective valve caps in place				
7. Empty or unused gas cylinders promptly returned to supplier				
H. Waste Disposal				
1. Containers kept sealed except during transfer				
2. Containers labeled with the words Hazardous Waste				
3. Constituents of the waste described on the container label				

4. Storage limited to < 1 quart of acutely hazardous waste				
5. Glass chemical containers recycled per established procedures				
6. Separate disposal containers available for broken glass				
7. Containers compatible with waste				

I. Training/Awareness

Training

1. Workers have attended hazard communication training				
2. Workers have attended emergency action plan training				
3. Workers have attended an orientation				
4. Workers have had training beyond EHS training				
5. Training (EHS and departmental) is documented				

Awareness: Do workers know:

1. What to do in the event of an emergency, such as fire, injury, including evacuation routes				
2. How to clean up chemical spills				
3. The Safety Manager for the department				
4. What an MSDS is and where to find them				
5. What type of personal protective equipment to use and when to use it				
6. What to do with chemical waste				

Facility Name

ACCIDENT/INCIDENT INVESTIGATION REPORT

FOR OFFICIAL USE ONLY

This document contains privileged, limited-use safety and privacy act–protected information. Unauthorized use or disclosure can subject you to criminal prosecution, termination of employment, civil liability, or other adverse actions.

Project Name:			Project Location:	
Completed By:		Date:	Accident Date:	Time:

Personal Injury		Property Damage	
Name:		Property Damaged:	
Employee no.:	Hire Date:	Nature of Damage:	

Performing Regular Job:
Type of Injury:
Nature of Injury:
Part of Body Injured:
Description of Accident: (What occurred? Include photos and diagram.)
Cause of Accident: (How and why did it occur? Documentation to support training.)
Witnesses: (Anyone who may have seen the accident occurred. Name, company, phone no.)
Corrective Actions: (Actions taken to prevent recurrence.)

Incident Investigation Report

Instructions: Complete this form as soon as possible after an incident that results in serious injury or illness. (Optional: Use to investigate a minor injury or near miss that *could have resulted in a serious injury or illness.*)

This is a report of a: ❑ Death ❑ Lost Time ❑ Dr. Visit Only ❑ First Aid Only ❑ Near Miss	
Date of incident:	This report is made by: ❑ Employee ❑ Supervisor ❑ Team ❑ Final Report

Step 1: Injured employee (complete this part for each injured employee)		
Name:	Sex: ❑ Male ❑ Female	Age:
Department:	Job title at time of incident:	
Part of body affected: (shade all that apply)	Nature of injury: (most serious one) ❑ Abrasion, scrapes ❑ Amputation ❑ Broken bone ❑ Bruise ❑ Burn (heat) ❑ Burn (chemical) ❑ Concussion (to the head) ❑ Crushing Injury ❑ Cut, laceration, puncture ❑ Hernia ❑ Illness ❑ Sprain, strain ❑ Damage to a body system: ❑ Other _____	This employee works: ❑ Regular full-time ❑ Regular part-time ❑ Seasonal ❑ Temporary
		Months with this employer:
		Months doing this job:
		(EG: nervous, respiratory, or circulatory systems)

Step 2: Describe the incident

Exact location of the incident:	Exact time:

What part of employee's workday?   Entering or leaving work   Doing normal work activities
     During meal period   During break   Working overtime   Other

Names of witnesses (if any):

Number of attachments:	Written witness statements:	Photographs:	Maps/drawings:

What personal protective equipment was being used (if any)?

Describe step-by-step, the events that led up to the injury. Include names of any machines, parts, objects, tools, materials, and other important details.

Step 3: Why did the incident happen?

Unsafe workplace conditions: (Check all that apply)	Unsafe acts by people: (Check all that apply)
❑ Inadequate guard	❑ Operating without permission
❑ Unguarded hazard	❑ Operating at unsafe speed
❑ Safety device is defective	❑ Servicing equipment that has power to it
❑ Tool or equipment defective	❑ Making a safety device inoperative
❑ Workstation layout is hazardous	❑ Using defective equipment
❑ Unsafe lighting	❑ Using equipment in an unapproved way
❑ Unsafe ventilation	❑ Unsafe lifting by hand
❑ Lack of needed personal protective equipment	❑ Taking an unsafe position or posture
❑ Lack of appropriate equipment/tools	❑ Distraction, teasing, horseplay
❑ Unsafe clothing	❑ Failure to wear personal protective equipment
❑ No training or insufficient training	❑ Failure to use the available equipment/tools
❑ Other: _____	❑ Other:

Why did the unsafe conditions exist?

Why did the unsafe acts occur?

Is there a reward (such as "the job can be done more quickly," or "the product is less likely to be damaged") that may have encouraged the unsafe conditions or acts? If yes, describe:	❑ Yes ❑ No
Were the unsafe acts or conditions reported prior to the incident?	❑ Yes ❑ No
Have there been similar incidents or near misses prior to this one?	❑ Yes ❑ No

Step 4: How can future incidents be prevented?

What changes do you suggest to prevent this injury/near-miss from happening again?

❑ Stop this activity   ❑ Guard the hazard   ❑ Train the employee(s) ❑ Train the supervisor(s)

❑ Redesign task steps ❑ Redesign workstation ❑ Write a new policy/rule ❑ Enforce existing policy

❑ Routinely inspect for the hazard ❑ Personal Protective Equipment ❑ Other:

What should be (or has been) done to carry out the suggestion(s) checked above?

Description continued on attached sheets: ❑

Step 5: Who completed and reviewed this form? (Please Print)	
Written by:	Title:
Department:	Date:
Names of investigation team members:	
Reviewed by:	Title:
	Date:

SUPERVISOR'S ACCIDENT/INCIDENT REPORT FORM

THIS FORM IS TO BE COMPLETED BY THE SUPERVISOR AND FORWARDED TO FACILITY MANAGER'S OFFICE WITH A WORKERS' COMPENSATION FORM AS SOON AS PRACTICABLE (or SEE HUMAN RESOURCES).

ALL ACCIDENTS INVOLVING SERIOUS BODILY INJURY OR DEATH MUST BE REPORTED TO THE FACILITY MANAGER'S OFFICE IMMEDIATELY.

ACCIDENT DATA

1. NAME OF EMPLOYEE:

2. ADDRESS AND PHONE NUMBER:

3. WORK DEPT. OR DIVISION: 4. SEX: 5.   DATE AND TIME OF INJURY
                                   MALE   FEMALE

6. NATURE OF INJURY: 7.   PART OF BODY INJURED:

8. CAUSE OF INJURY: 9.   LOCATION OF ACCIDENT:

10. OCCUPATION OF PERSON AT TIME OF ACCIDENT: 11.   STATUS OF JOB :
                                                 HALTED   CONTINUED   COMPLETED

12. NAME AND PHONE NO. OF ACCIDENT WITNESSES: (BEFORE, DURING, OR AFTERWARD)

13. LIST UNSAFE ACT, IF ANY:

14. LIST UNSAFE PHYSICAL OR MECHANICAL CONDITION, IF ANY:

15. UNSAFE PERSONAL FACTOR:

16. LIST HAZARD CONTROLS IN EFFECT AT TIME OF INJURY DESIGNED TO PREVENT INJURY:

17. PERSONAL PROTECTIVE EQUIPMENT BEING USED AT TIME OF ACCIDENT:
    GLOVES, SAFETY GLASSES, GOGGLES, FACE-SHIELD, OTHER:

18. BRIEF DESCRIPTION OF ACCIDENT:

19. CORRECTIVE ACTION TAKEN OR RECOMMENDED BY SUPERVISOR:

TREATMENT DATA

20. WAS INJURED TAKEN TO: (CIRCLE ONE) HOSPITAL FAMILY PRACTICE CENTER HOME

21. DIAGNOSIS AND TREATMENT, IF KNOWN:

22. ESTIMATED LOST WORKDAYS (EXCLUDING DAY OF ACCIDENT):

23. REPORT PREPARED BY: 24.   DATE OF REPORT:

Confined-Space Entry Permit
Job Location

Location and Description of Confined Space:

_____

Purpose of Entry: _____ Responsible Dept: _____

_____

Date (mm/dd/yyyy): _____/_____/_____ Time: _____ Expiration:
_____/_____/_____

Phone Numbers

Project Supervisor: _____

Other Emergency Numbers: _____

Responsible Individuals

Supervisor(s) / Project Manager(s)	Authorized Entrants	Authorized Attendants

Special Requirements

Lock-out/Tag-out Complete	Yes ☐ No ☐	Escape harness	Yes ☐	No ☐
Lines Broken: Capped or Blanked	Yes ☐ No ☐	Tripod	Yes ☐	No ☐
Purge: Flush or Inert	Yes ☐ No ☐	Life Lines	Yes ☐	No ☐
Ventilation: 30 Min. in Advance	Yes ☐ No ☐	Fire Extinguishers	Yes ☐	No ☐
Secure Area: Signs Barriers	Yes ☐ No ☐	Breathing Apparatus	Yes ☐	No ☐
Lighting (Explosion Proof)	Yes ☐ No ☐	Protective Clothing	Yes ☐	No ☐
Location of Emergency Phone	Yes ☐ No ☐	Respirator (Air-Purifying)	Yes ☐	No ☐

Atmospheric Testing	Limits	Time	Time	Time	Time	Time	Time	Time
Oxygen (%)	19.5 to 23.5							
LEL (%)	> 10%							
Carbon Monoxide (CO)	25 ppm							

Atmospheric Testing

Instruments Used:	Type:	Serial # :

Technician's Name:

_____

Authorization
Authorized Supervisor:

_____

Signature:

_____

Date (mm/dd/yyyy): _____/_____/_____ Time: _____

Lock-out/Tag-out Form   Facilities Management Work Order No.:

Description of Machine/Equipment
or Work:
_____

Building: _____ Room #: _____

Start Date: _____ End Date: _____

Lock No.	Employee Name	Start Date/Signature	End Date/Signature

---

Lock-Out/Tag-Out (LOTO) Devices (e.g., locks, chains, clamps, etc.)

The following steps need to be performed to safely place, remove, and transfer LOTO devices to energy-isolating devices:
1. Notify all affected personnel (operators of machine equipment, etc) that LOTO procedures are in effect.
2. Identify and isolate energy sources
3. Lock and tag
4. Test the controls
5. Perform the work
6. Remove locks and tags

Re-Energizing Equipment/Machine
Before startup of machine/equipment after servicing, complete the following steps:

1. Make sure machine/equipment is in good working order.
2. Notify all affected personnel that LOTO devices are being removed from equipment/machinery and all personnel are safely positioned away from the equipment/machinery.
3. Check for and retrieve all loose tools, equipment, and machine parts. Reinstall all removed equipment/machine guards.
4. Remove all LOTO devices from energy isolating devices.
5. Operate the energy-isolating devices to restore energy to the equipment/machine.

Name: _____

Send 1 copy at the end of job to the Immediate Supervisor and another to the Facility Manager.

_____

Appendix E

Safety Glossary and List of Acronyms and Abbreviations

Abate: to eliminate or reduce permanently an unsafe or unhealthful working condition by coming into compliance with the applicable OSHA standard

Abrasive-blasting Respirator: a continuous-flow airline respirator constructed so that it will cover the wearer's head, neck, and shoulders and protect the wearer from abrasive and other related materials

Accident Investigation: the investigation conducted into the facts surrounding the causes of an accident

ACGIH: American Conference of Government Industrial Hygienists

Acid: any corrosive having a pH less than 7

ACM: Asbestos-Containing Material

Acute: a single exposure to a toxic substance which may result in severe biological harm or death; an acute exposure occurs over a comparatively short track

ADA: Americans with Disabilities Act

Administrative Control: any procedure which limits daily exposures to toxic chemicals or harmful physical agents by managing the work schedule

ANSI: American National Standards Institute; a national consensus standard-developing organization

APF: Assigned Protection Factor

Asbestos: a fibrous mineral that can be produced into a material that is fireproof and possesses high tensile strength, good heat, and electrical insulating capabilities, and moderate to good chemical resistance; inhalation of dust poses a severe health hazard

Atmosphere Immediately Dangerous to Life or Health (IDLH): the concentration of a contaminant which can produce an immediate irreversible, debilitating effect on health, or which can cause death

Base: any corrosive having a pH greater than 7

Baseline Monitoring: periodic examination of blood, urine, or any other body substance to determine exposure to toxic substances

Baseline Survey: initial survey to identify hazardous workplace conditions or unsafe work practices

BLS: Bureau of Labor Statistics

CAA: Clean Air Act (1955, 1977, and 1990): federal law mandating and enforcing toxic emission standards for stationary sources and motor vehicles

Cartridge, Air-Purifying (for Respirator): a container with a filter, sorbent, or catalyst or any combination of these which removes specific contaminants from the air drawn through it

Causes: conditions or events explaining why a mishap occurred

Caustic: any corrosive having a pH greater than 7

Caution Tag: tag used as precautionary notification to indicate that caution must be exercised in operating tagged equipment

CERCLA: Comprehensive Environmental Responsibility, Compensation, and Liability Act (1980, 1986), also known as the Superfund Legislation

CFR: Code of Federal Regulations; the general and permanent rules published in the Federal Register by the executive departments and agencies of the federal government

Chronic: persistent, prolonged, repeated

Combustible Liquid: any liquid having a flash point at or above 100 degrees Fahrenheit, but below 200 degrees Fahrenheit (except any mixture having components with flash points of 200 degrees Fahrenheit or higher, the total volume of which make up 99 percent or more of the total volume of the mixture)

Compressed Gas: material, which may or may not be hazardous material in itself, that is stored in pressurized containers

Concentration: the quantity of a substance per unit volume (in appropriate units); examples of concentration units provided below:

- **mg/m3:** milligrams per cubic meter for vapors, gases, fumes, or dusts
- **ppm:** parts per million for vapors or gases
- **fibers/cc:** fibers per cubic centimeter for asbestos

Confined Space: a compartment such as a tank, boiler, furnace, or void, which because of its small size, limited access, or confined nature can readily create, aggravate, or result in a hazardous condition due to the presence of toxic gases or lack of oxygen

Contaminant: a material that is not normally present in the atmosphere, which can be harmful, irritating, or a nuisance to anyone who breathes it

Corrosive Material: any hazardous material that will cause severe tissue damage by chemical action or materially damage surfaces or cause a fire when in contact with organic material or certain other chemicals

CWA: Clean Water Act (1972); federal law regulating discharge of pollutants into surface waters

Danger Tag: tag prohibiting operation of equipment that endangers safety of personnel, equipment, systems, or components

Decibel-dB: a unit used to express sound pressure levels; in hearing testing, the unit used to express hearing threshold levels as referred to audiometric zero

DEP: Department of Environmental Protection

Detector Tube: a glass tube which utilizes a sensitive chemical (in a suspension of silica gel) which produces color change whenever contaminated air is pulled through the tube

DHS: Department of Homeland Security

Disabling Work/Injury: any impairment resulting from an accident or occupational disease which prevents a person from performing his regularly established duty or work

DOL: Department of Labor

Dosimeter: a device for measuring cumulatively the ionizing radiation exposure of an individual over a period of time

DOT: Department of Transportation

Dust: small solid particles created by the breaking up of larger particles by processes such as crushing, grinding, or explosion; examples of processes that generate dust: use of machine shop tools, paint chipping, sanding, woodworking, abrasive blasting

EEBD (Emergency Escape Breathing Device): a respirator that provides the user with oxygen through a chemical reaction; used only for emergency escape procedures

EHS: Environmental Health and Safety

EMS: Environmental Management System

EMT: Emergency Medical Technician

EPA: Environmental Protection Agency

FERT: Facility Emergency Response Team

First Aid: any one-time treatment, any follow-up visit for the purpose of observation, of minor scratches, cuts, burns, splinters, and so forth, which do not ordinarily require medical care; such one-time treatment and follow-up visit for the purpose of observation is considered first aid even though provided by a physician or other licensed health care professional personnel

Flammable Liquid: any liquid having a flash point less than 100 degrees Fahrenheit

Flammable Liquids Cabinet: a cabinet specifically designed and authorized for storing flammable in-use material

Flammable Liquids Storeroom: a space specifically designed and authorized for storing flammable liquids

Flash Point: the minimum temperature of a flammable liquid at which it gives off sufficient vapor to form an ignitable mixture with air near the surface of the liquid

FM: Factory Mutual (an organization of a group of insurers composed of mutual property and casualty insurance companies, a subsidiary stock insurance company and a subsidiary safety engineering company)

FRA: First Responder Awareness

Frequency: the rate at which a sound source vibrates or makes the air vibrate determines frequency; the unit of time usually one second and the term hertz (Hz) used to designate the number of cycles per second; frequency related to the subjective sensation of pitch; high frequency sounds (2000, 3000, and 4000 hz) are high pitched

Friable Asbestos: loosely bound asbestos whose fibers may easily crumble or pulverize; a health hazard because it easily releases contaminants into the air

Fume: very small particles (1 micrometer or less) formed by the condensation of volatilized solids, usually metals; examples of processes that generate fumes: smelting, furnace work, foundry operations, and welding

FWPCA: Federal Water Pollution Control Act

Gas: a material that under normal conditions of temperature and pressure tends to occupy the entire space uniformly

Hazard: a condition which might result in injury, illness, disease, or death to anyone exposed to the condition, or which might result in damage to or loss of material, equipment, or systems; people detect hazards through inspections, surveys, observations of near-miss incidents, safety program evaluations, or from reports by others

Hazard Abatement Log: a record of identified deficiencies in chronological order by department, area, or facility

Hazard Severity: an assessment of the worst potential consequence which is likely to occur as a result of deficiencies

Hazardous Material (HM): any material that because of its quantity, concentration, or physical or chemical characteristics may pose a substantial hazard to human health or the environment when purposefully released or accidentally spilled; definition includes:

- Aerosol containers
- Flammable materials
- Toxic materials
- Corrosive materials (including acids)
- Oxidizing materials
- Compressed gases

Hazardous Waste (HW): any material (liquid, solid, or gas) which meets the above definition of hazardous material and is not used, stored, transported properly, or is spent (used) and/or is designated as a hazardous waste by the Environmental Protection Agency or a state hazardous material control authority

HAZCOM: Hazard Communication (also, 29 CFR 1910.1200)

HAZMAT: Hazardous material(s)

HAZWOPER: Hazardous Waste Operations and Emergency Response

Hearing Level: amounts in decibels by which the threshold of audition for an ear differs from zero decibels (dB) for each frequency; a standard audiometric threshold derived from normal-hearing young adults

Heat Exhaustion: a heat illness caused by salt depletion and dehydration, which is evidenced by profuse sweating, headache, nausea, vomiting, tingling sensations, leading to unconsciousness

Heat Stress: any combination of air temperature, thermal radiation, humidity, air flow, and work load that may stress the body as it attempts to regulate body temperature; heat stress becomes excessive when the body's capability to adjust is exceeded, resulting in an increase of body temperature

Heat Stroke: heat illness where the thermo-regulatory system fails to function, so the main avenue of heat loss is blocked resulting in unconsciousness, convulsions, delirium, and possible death.

Hertz (hz): unit of frequency

HM: hazardous material

HMIS: Hazardous Material Information System

HMTUSA: Hazardous Materials Transportation Uniform Safety Act

HS: hazardous substance

HW: hazardous waste

ICS: Incident Command System

IDLH: Immediately Dangerous to Life or Health; the concentration of a contaminant atmosphere that can produce an immediate irreversible debilitating effect on health, or that can cause death

IH: Industrial Hygienist; person trained in industrial hygiene; may be assigned as safety officer

Illness: any abnormal condition or disorder, other than one resulting from an injury, caused by exposure to conditions associated with the occupational environment

Imminent Danger: a condition that immediately threatens the loss of life or serious injury or illness of an employee

Impulse or Impact Noise: sound of short duration, usually less than one second, with an abrupt onset and rapid decay

Incompatible HM/HW: any materials that react with each other to produce undesirable products; mixing incompatible hazardous material can produce heat or pressure, fire or explosion, or toxic, irritating, or flammable dusts, mists, fumes, or gases

Industrial Hygiene: the science that deals with the recognition, evaluation, and control of potential health hazards in the work environment

Injury: traumatic bodily harm, such as a cut, fracture, burn, or poisoning, caused by a single or one-day exposure to an external force, toxic substance, or physical agent

Inspection: careful and critical workplace monitoring for safety hazards and deficiencies; ensures that standards are being observed

Ionizing Radiation: radiation with sufficient energy to strip electrons from atoms in the media through which it passes; examples include alpha particles, beta particles, and X- and gamma rays

Isolation: the physical separation of a hazard from potential personnel contact by the use of a barrier or other means

Laser: a device which generates coherent electromagnetic radiation in the ultraviolet, visible, or infrared regions of the spectrum

LEPC: Local Emergency Planning Committees

Lost Workday Case: a reportable lost-time case is one preventing a person from performing regular duty or work on the day of injury or onset of work-related illness

LOTO: Lock-Out/Tag-Out

Material Safety Data Sheet (MSDS): written or printed data concerning an HM prepared by the manufacturer of the HM in accordance with paragraph (g) of 29 CFR 1910.1200 (Hazard Communication Standard)

Medical Surveillance: an effort to monitor the health of individuals for job certification/ recertification, for ensuring the effectiveness of hazard limiting programs, for indication of excessive exposure in the workplace, and for compliance with some of the OSHA standards

Medical Treatment: treatment administered by a physician or by registered personnel under the standing orders of a physician; medical treatment does not include first-aid treatment even though provided by a physician or licensed healthcare professional personnel

Mist and Fog: finely divided liquid droplets suspended in air and generated by condensation or atomization; fog is a mist of sufficient concentration to obscure vision; examples of materials and processes that produce mists: acid sprays used in metal treatment (for example, electroplating, organic solvent sprays, and spray painting)

Monitoring (Industrial Hygiene): measurement of the amount of contaminant or physical stress reaching the worker in the environment; also referred to as workplace monitoring

Monitoring (Medical Surveillance): the preplacement and periodic evaluation of body functions to ascertain the health status of personnel exposed to significant concentrations of toxic substances (for example, decreased lung function, dermatitis, abnormal blood count) allowing early detection of adverse health effects on the individual

Monitoring Hearing Tests: periodic hearing tests, obtained subsequent to the reference hearing test, which are used to detect shifts in the individual's threshold of hearing

MSHA: Mine Safety and Health Administration

MUC: Maximum use concentration

Near Miss: an act or event which could have resulted in an accident, but chance alone averted injury, death, or damage

NFPA: National Fire Protection Association

NIOSH: National Institute for Occupational Safety and Health

NIOSH/MSHA Certified Equipment: respirators or other equipment that have been tested by NIOSH or MSHA and jointly approved as meeting certain minimum requirements of protection against specified hazards

Noise Exposure: personal interaction to a combination of effective sound level and its duration

Nonionizing Radiation: radiation that is not capable of stripping electrons from atoms in the media through which it passes; examples include radio waves, microwaves, visible light, and ultraviolet radiation

NPDES: National Pollutant Discharge Elimination System

NRC (National Response Center): established under the National Contingency Plan to provide information regarding emergency response actions during oil or hazardous substances spills or releases; phone 24 hours/day 1-800-424-8802

Occupational Health: the multidisciplinary field of general preventative medicine that is concerned with the prevention and/or treatment of illness induced by factors in the workplace environment; major disciplines involved are: occupational medicine, occupational health nursing, epidemiology, toxicology, industrial hygiene, and health physics

OJT: On-the-job training

OSC: On-Scene Coordinator

OSHA: Occupational Safety and Health Administration, Department of Labor

OSHA Standards: OSHA standards are those standards issued by the Department of Labor's Occupational Safety and Health Administration pursuant to the OSHAct

OSHAct: The Williams-Steiger Occupational Safety and Health Act of 1970

Oxidizers: any material that readily yields oxygen for combustion

Oxygen Deficient Atmosphere: atmosphere with insufficient oxygen (O_2) to support life; deficiency is generally caused by oxidation, dilution, or displacement of oxygen by other gases; > 19.5 percent oxygen, per OSHA

Particulate Matter: any fine solid or liquid particles such as dust, fog, fumes, mist, smoke, or spray; particulate matter suspended in air is commonly known as an aerosol

PCB: Polychlorinated Biphenyl

PEL (Permissible Exposure Limit): the legally established time-weighted average (TWA) concentration or ceiling concentration of a contaminant or exposure level of a harmful physical agent that shall not be exceeded

Personal Protective Equipment (PPE): a device or item to be worn, used, or put in place for the safety or protection of an individual or the public at large, when performing work assignments or in entering hazardous areas or under hazardous conditions; equipment includes hard hats, safety glasses, hearing protection, respirators, electrical matting, barricades, traffic cones, lights, safety lines, and life jackets.

Pesticide: any chemical used to kill pests, such as insects

PPE: Personal Protective Equipment

ppm: parts per million

Protective Clothing: an article of clothing furnished to an employee at the employer's expense and worn for personal safety and protection in the performance of work assignments in potentially hazardous areas or under hazardous conditions

Qualitative Fit–Testing: a simple procedure of fitting an individual with a respirator face mask

Quantitative Fit-Testing: respirator fit-test procedure involving the use of a special enclosure filled with sodium chloride mist or other chemicals, a sensor attached to the mask to be tested, and a monitoring device to detect leakage of the chemical into the mask.

Radiation Safety Officer: a person assigned to be the technical manager of the facility's radiation protection program

RCRA: Resource Conservation and Recovery Act

REL: Recommended Exposure Limits

Respirator: device used for protecting the respiratory tract from harmful contaminants

Safety: freedom from those conditions that can cause death, injury, occupational illness, or damage to or loss of equipment on property

Safety Committee: a committee consisting of the safety officer, as well as other members of management and the workforce. Identifies and discusses safety-related problems, enhances interdepartmental communication in accident prevention, and submits issues and recommendations to senior management; should meet at least quarterly

Safety Data File: the computer file used to store the hazardous material characteristics relevant to their safe handling, use, and disposal

SARA: Superfund Amendments and Reauthorization Act

SARA Title III: Superfund Amendments and Reauthorization Act Title III (Emergency Planning and Community Right-To-Know Act)

SCP: Spill Contingency Plan

Self-Contained Breathing Apparatus (SCBA): breathing apparatus where compressed air is carried in a tank on the user's back

SERC: State Emergency Response Commission

Serious Physical Harm: permanent, prolonged, or temporary impairment of the body in which part of the body is made functionally useless or is substantially reduced in efficiency on or off the job; illness could shorten life or significantly reduce physical or mental efficiency by inhibiting the normal function of part of the body; examples of such illnesses are silicosis, asbestosis, hearing impairment, radiation exposure, and visual impairment

Solvent: a substance, most commonly water, but often an organic compound which is used to dissolve another substance

Standard: a rule, established by a competent authority, which designates safe and healthful conditions or practices under which work must be performed to prevent injury, occupational illness, or property damage

STEL: Short-Term Exposure Levels

Substitution: the risk of injury or illness may be reduced by replacement of an existing process, material, or equipment with a similar item having a lower hazard potential

Supervisor: one who immediately directs the job efforts of a working group or individual

Survey: an examination of the condition of industrial hygiene and occupational health of a command; examination is often, but not always, performed by industrial hygienists or technicians under the supervision of an industrial hygienist

Time-Weighted Average (TWA): the average concentration of a contaminant in air during a specific period of time, usually an eight-hour workday or a 40-hour work week

TLV (Threshold Limit Value): an atmospheric exposure level under which nearly all workers can work without harmful effects; TLVs are established by the American Conference of Governmental Industrial Hygienists (ACGIH)

Toxic Material: a substance which when ingested, inhaled, or absorbed through the skin in sufficient amounts can produce harmful effects, such as changes in living tissue, impairment of the central nervous system, severe illness, or, in extreme cases, death

Transportation Data File: the computer file used to store the hazardous material characteristics relevant to their safe transportation and handling

TSCA: Toxic Substance Control Act

TSDF: Treatment, storage, and disposal facilities

UN: United Nations

Vapor: the gaseous state of a substance that is normally a liquid or solid at room temperature; examples of substances that produce vapors: degreasers, fuels, hydraulic fluids, paints and thinners, and dry-cleaning fluids

Variances: when and if an OSHA standard is found to be impossible to comply with, variances (temporary or permanent) can be requested from OSHA, in writing; variance requests shall explain why compliance is impossible and describe actions taken to achieve the maximum degree of protection possible; the employees must be informed of the variance request

Ventilation: the control of potentially hazardous airborne substances through the movement of air

WBGT Index: a measurement of environmental conditions (heat stress); consists of a weighted average of dry-bulb, wet-bulb, and globe temperatures

WBGT Meter: instrument used for measuring heat stress; measures dry-bulb, wet-bulb, and globe temperatures and integrates these values into the WBGT index

Workplace Monitoring: the evaluation of a workplace to accurately identify and quantify all potential hazards; this will consist of routine inspections and industrial hygiene surveys

Index

abandoned facilities, contamination from, 33–34

accident investigations, 131; report form, 202–210

accidents: instruction in preventing, 164; occupational, 132–33; supervisor's report form for, 131, 202–7; testing after, *132*

ACGIH. *See* American Conference of Governmental Industrial Hygienists

ACM. *See* asbestos-containing materials

ADA. *See* Americans with Disabilities Act

air: compressor, 146–47; quality, 21

airborne hazardous substances, 62

Air Quality Act of 1967, 32

American Conference of Governmental Industrial Hygienists (ACGIH), 115

American Society of Industrial Security (ASIS), 69

Americans with Disabilities Act (ADA), 24; compliant sign, *24*

annual safety audit form, 178–79

APFs. *See* assigned protection factors

asbestos: contractor, *104*; as fireproofing material, *101*; in-place management of, 103; OSHA standard, 55, 103; products containing, *102–3*; safety inspection checklist, 175; sign, *105*; warning notices, 103

asbestos-containing materials (ACM), 103; label, *104*; location of, 105

ASIS. *See* American Society of Industrial Security

assigned protection factors (APFs), 39, 63–64; respirators, *64*

audit forms: annual safety, 176–78; chemical use in facility areas, 195–98; confined space entry, 178–79; electrical safety, 180–83; fire prevention, 184; flammable liquid storage, 185–86; LOTO, 187–88; personal protective equipment, 189–90; respiratory protection, 191

barricade, 164

Bhopal, India, 36

BLS. *See* Bureau of Labor Statistics

British Standard BS 7750, 82

Bureau of Labor Statistics (BLS), 20

business continuity plan, 67; cycle, *68*

CAA. *See* Clean Air Act

Catastrophic/Fatal Accident inspections, 22

CEO. *See* Chief Executive Officers

CERCLA. *See* Comprehensive Environmental Response Compensation and Liability Act

Certified Protection Professional (CPP), 69

CFR. *See* Code of Federal Regulations

chain saw, 146, *147*

chemical facilities, 77, *78*; audit form, 197–201; inventory lists for, 37

Chemical Hazard Response Information System (CHRIS), 49

Chief Executive Officers (CEO), 66; responsibilities of, 125

CHRIS. *See* Chemical Hazard Response Information System

Clean Air Act (CAA), 32

cleaning products, 87

Clean Water Act, 30

closure sign, *74*

Code of Federal Regulations (CFR), 28

About the Author

Brian J. Gallant has an associate's degree in fire science and safety, a bachelor's in management, and a master's in education. He spent twelve years in the fire service, serving as training officer, hazardous material officer, department fire investigator, and shift commander (fire lieutenant). Mr. Gallant served as an instructor with the Massachusetts Firefighting Academy's Industrial Fire Training Program, specializing in both marine and nuclear firefighting. He was also the director of fire training for Barnstable County, Massachusetts, encompassing twenty communities on Cape Cod.

Mr. Gallant served as the emergency management director for the town of Sandwich, and under his regime, handled several major (high-profile) incidents. Among them included two powerful hurricanes, a "no-name" storm, and a barge accident in the Cape Cod Canal area involving hazardous materials and then potential evacuation of a large seasonal section of the community.

He was recruited from the fire department to a large nuclear power facility and became a training supervisor, responsible for fire, hazardous materials, safety evaluation, and several other training programs. From the nuclear industry, he went to California to become the regional manager of a full-service environmental consulting firm.

Mr. Gallant is currently vice president of Contingency Management Associates, Inc., and is responsible for all environmental, health, and safety training and consulting activities for the Massachusetts-based firm. He has serviced clients worldwide.

He serves as an instructor at Massachusetts Maritime Academy, lecturing in the areas of health and safety, emergency management, OPA 90 training, STCW, and marina management, as well as several other courses.

Mr. Gallant serves as an associate with a major spill management team. As such, he performs the duties as safety officer at marine and hazardous material–related incidents and casualties. He has served as safety/security consultant at several major responses. Additionally, he has trained several marine-related clients and acted as safety officer in drills and exercises.

Mr. Gallant is a member of the Barnstable County Deputy Sheriff's Association, the National Association of Fire Investigators, and the American Society of Safety Engineers, and is a Certified Hazardous Material Manager.